Content and Language Integrated Learning by Interaction

FOREIGN LANGUAGE PEDAGOGY
CONTENT- AND LEARNER-ORIENTED

Edited by Gabriele Blell and Rita Kupetz
Co-founded by Karlheinz Hellwig

VOLUME 26

Zu Qualitätssicherung und Peer Review der vorliegenden Publikation

Die Qualität der in dieser Reihe erscheinenden Arbeiten wird vor der Publikation durch beide Herausgeberinnen der Reihe geprüft.

Notes on the quality assurance and peer review of this publication

Prior to publication, the quality of the work published in this series is reviewed by both editors of the series.

Rita Kupetz / Carmen Becker (eds)

Content and Language Integrated Learning by Interaction

PETER LANG
EDITION

Bibliographic Information published by the Deutsche Nationalbibliothek
The Deutsche Nationalbibliothek lists this publication in the Deutsche Nationalbibliografie; detailed bibliographic data is available in the internet at http://dnb.d-nb.de.

Library of Congress Cataloging-in-Publication Data
Content and language integrated learning by interaction / Kupetz, Rita ; Becker, Carmen (eds).
pages cm. — (Foreign language pedagogy - content- and learner-oriented; Band 26)
ISBN 978-3-631-64899-5
1. Language and languages—Study and teaching—Psychological aspects. 2. Cognitive learning. 3. Language and languages—Computer-assisted . 4. Human-computer interaction. 5. Language experience approach in education. I. Kupetz, Rita, editor of compilation. II. Becker, Carmen, editor of compilation.
P53.7.C66 2014
418.0071—dc23

2014000370

ISSN 1430-8150
ISBN 978-3-631-64899-5 (Print)
E-ISBN 978-3-653-04725-7 (E-Book)
DOI 10.3726/978-3-653-04725-7

© Peter Lang GmbH
Internationaler Verlag der Wissenschaften
Frankfurt am Main 2014
All rights reserved.
Peter Lang Edition is an Imprint of Peter Lang GmbH.

Peter Lang – Frankfurt am Main · Bern · Bruxelles · New York · Oxford · Warszawa · Wien

This publication has been peer reviewed.

www.peterlang.com

Contents

Preface

Rita Kupetz and Carmen Becker, Leibniz Universität Hannover, Germany

Content and Language Integrated Learning (CLIL) is an established approach to support multilingualism by teaching various school subjects in an additional European language. The methodology, the procedures and the educational strategies used, however, vary considerably (Dalton-Puffer, 2011: 9), and so do the results (Ruiz de Zarobe et al., 2011). Our book considers this diversity by looking at CLIL scenarios, defined as learning environments supporting content learning, language learning and learning skill development, probably in a task-based learning setting, with a strong focus on interaction (Coyle, 2011: 68) in different curricular contexts and at various levels of proficiency. CLIL by Interaction is understood both as negotiation of meaning and form and as discourse with a CLIL learner to empower him or her to participate in social discourse (Bonnet, 2013: 189).

The curricular contexts are related to the editors' academic network which is based at the Leibniz Universität Hannover (Germany) and related to schools in this region, where the editors collaborate with Alexander Woltin, a teacher of English and biology, who provides both a linguistic and a content-oriented perspective on CLIL. Peer-to-peer scaffolding is studied in a poster project carried out in a primary school science class by Carmen Becker using interaction analysis. A more linguistic perspective is shown in the research on interaction analysis in teacher education, carried out by Rita Kupetz together with Maxi Kupetz from Potsdam University. The collaboration with Ivana Marenzi from the research centre L3S in Hannover led to a study on CLIL material design in teacher education using the search-and-share capabilities of new technologies. Jana Roos completes this volume by investigating communicative tasks in CLIL learning scenarios at secondary school.

The book employs linguistic approaches such as interaction analysis and educational assumptions such as a constructivist approach to learning, design-based research or a case-based approach to learning, where CLIL scenarios are recorded and studied. The goal in all of these investigations is to recognize linguistic and pedagogic patterns, such as scaffolding, code-switching and repair, and their relevance for specific activities in CLIL interaction.

One major focus is on how classroom interaction analysis can make a difference in teacher education and ongoing professional development (Escobar Urmeneta, 2013). CLIL teacher education has changed in Germany from sporadic (Blell, Kupetz, 2005) to a more systematic approach covering all three phases of teacher education from university to on-the-job training (Gnutzmann, Rabe, 2013). The approach used at Leibniz Universität Hannover is characterized by its curricular contextualization in foreign language teacher education and a more and more intensified collaboration with teacher students' second subject methodology, such as teaching history (in English) or teaching geography (in English).

Interaction is also described in the context of designing CLIL material, focusing in particular on communication and collaboration, and how the search-and-share capabilities of new technologies greatly facilitate the development of students' conceptual understanding and procedural competence.

In sum, the CLIL research presented in this volume sheds light on CLIL from a predominantly linguistic perspective – interaction analysis in collaboration with subject teachers and an educational perspective – covering the concepts of multiliteracies, task-based learning and IT-enhanced learning.

Acknowledgements

Thank you to all the contributors, to René Uckert for the technical support and, last but not least, to our students involved in the research.

References

Blell, Gabriele, Kupetz, Rita (eds) (2005). *Bilingualer Sachfachunterricht und Lehrerausbildung für den Bilingualen Unterricht. Forschung und Praxisberichte*. Frankfurt am Main: Peter Lang.

Bonnet, Andreas (2013). 'Unterrichtsprozesse', in Wolfgang Hallet and Frank G. Königs (eds), pp.187-94.

Breidbach, Stephan, Viebrock, Britta (2012). 'CLIL in Germany – results from recent research in a contested field of education', *International CLIL Research Journal* 1, 4: 5-16.

Coyle, Do (2011). 'Post-method pedagogies: using a second or other language as a learning tool in CLIL settings', in Yolanda Ruiz de Zarobe et al. (eds), pp. 49-73.

Dalton-Puffer, Christiane (2011). 'Foreword', in Yolanda Ruiz de Zarobe et al. (eds), pp. 9-10.

Escobar Urmeneta, Cristina (2013). 'Learning to become a CLIL teacher: teaching, reflection and professional development', *International Journal of Bilingual Education and Bilingualism* 16, 3: 334-53.

Gnutzmann, Claus, Rabe, Frank (2013). 'Bilingualer Unterricht: Lehrerbildung in der 1., 2. und 3. Phase', in Wolfgang Hallet and Frank G. Königs (eds), pp. 102-10.

Hallet, Wolfgang, Königs, Frank G. (eds) (2013). *Handbuch Bilingualer Unterricht. Content and Language Integrated Learning.* Seelze: Klett & Kallmeyer.

Ruiz de Zarobe, Yolanda et al. (eds) (2011). *Content and Foreign Language Integrated Learning. Contributions to multilingualism in European contexts.* Bern: Peter Lang.

Language education policy and CLIL principles

Rita Kupetz and Alexander Woltin, Leibniz Universität Hannover, Germany

1. CLIL and education policy

The first bilingual programmes in Germany arose from post-war cooperation efforts between Germany and France (the Élysée Contract). These programmes focused on a partnership by developing the target language as the language of the partner. Thus, the German bilingual programme has a past of strong linguistic and intercultural emphasis due to socio-historical reasons back in 1963. This focus has changed over the last 50 years because the plurilingual background of the learners, who are partially or fully bilingual, had to be considered as well (Lyster, 2007: 1, Bongartz, Rymarczyk, 2010: 7f., Breidbach, Viehbrock, 2012: 10f., Königs, 2013: 34f.). Consequently, more languages are now involved in bilingual teaching settings, due to a diverse learner and teacher clientele. The potential for multilingualism is central since language policies desire that students acquire two foreign languages in addition to their first language (L1) (Wolff, 2013: 18). The re-cognition of the importance of the L1 in all learning processes, which could be the home language for students with migration backgrounds, is a part of this new orientation, which is discussed in detail in the context of the Canadian language situation, where territorial bilingualism occurs (Wesche, 2002, Swain, Lapkin, 2005). Bilingual branches teaching content in a foreign language at school level have been offered in Germany since the 1960s, and Content and Language Integrated Learning (CLIL) has been popular since the 1990s in Europe as an approach which integrates teaching content in the foreign, second or additional language learning, where the additional language is used as a medium for authentic usage (Marsh, 2002).

Vollmer (2006: 5f.) discusses CLIL's potential in terms of internal and external processes of plurilingualism in the context of Europe:

> Acquiring conceptual literacy and discourse competence for subject-specific use and thus acquiring new varieties of language use within one and the same language is not to be seen as a luxury, but rather as a *preliminary and fundamental form of plurilingualism*.
>
> A *second form of plurilingualism* develops when a learner acquires other languages, extends his/her repertoire with new languages *through foreign language education* adding to the new varieties of the language of school education and home

language if different. Both types of plurilingualism (the first discourse-based or *internal* one as well as the second *external* one, based on adding new language repertoires) are indispensable for learners to become intra-culturally and inter-culturally sensitive, knowledgeable and skilled and thus to develop towards democratic citizenship and participation within Europe. A special case in point concerns the integration of content and second language learning within the framework of CLIL (or multilingual education) leading ideally to support for both types of plurilingualism.

A desired global aim and imperative in a world becoming increasingly interconnected and interdependent through globalization (Wolff, 2000: 159) is the acquisition of multi-literal and intra- as well as inter-cultural competences. These competences unite important sensitive abilities, namely plurilingual and democratic participation as a part of global education, which focuses on the awareness and implications of dealing with global issues (O'Loughlin, Wegimont, 2002: 126). Lyster (2007: 1) points out similar changes around the world based on social and linguistic demographics, which lead to "a continued need to develop more effective second language programs to meet the changing needs of local communities." In short, education ought to promote globally competent life-long learners. Since each and every subject teaches its subject specifically, and interdisciplinary methods including various literacies and content cannot be acquired without language and vice versa (Hallet, 2005: 5, Vollmer, 2013: 125), educators refer to this teaching approach as Language Across the Curriculum (LAC) (Vollmer, 2006: 5, Lyster, 2007: 56). Further, this approach clearly indicates every teacher's responsibility for holistic language education, thus making purely bilingual education no longer appropriate. The term is even worth reconsidering. Content, languages and methods must be fused to meet the multicultural premises of the diverse learners (Hallet, 2013: 54) as well as to meet the goals of global education in terms of globally competent and multiliterate life-long learners.

Ruiz de Zarobe et al. (2011: 13) discuss the plurilingual perspective offered by CLIL and claim that it is "one of the most effective frameworks to foster plurilingualism in the European landscape, where it is firmly becoming a preferred educational approach." However, CLIL practice in Europe is characterized by diversity, both in terms of language policy and the instructional approaches used at school (Königs, 2013: 48ff.).

2. A counterbalanced approach to CLIL in a global education framework

Researchers, mainly second language (L2) researchers, have investigated the learning processes involved in recent years leading to a theoretical turn in the CLIL community (Bonnet, Breidbach, 2004). Doff (2010: 12) argues that there was a bottom-up approach from teaching practice to empirical research in the 1990s. However, the current development is closer to a theoretical takeover.

Bilingual branches and immersion programmes are very popular with politicians, parents and students alike. The German-English competence study (DESI) (Nold et al., 2008), comparing the competences of 9th graders in German and English in Germany, shows that CLIL students are about two years ahead of language learners taught in conventional foreign language classes. The study clearly indicates higher competence within the fields of text reconstruction, listening and reading comprehension, grammar, writing and socio-pragmatic issues. The best results within these areas can be observed in the CLIL students' listening and grammar competences. It can be assumed that this is the result of frequent L2 exposure and, thus, learning time within an authentic and communicative CLIL environment.

With regards to CLIL discourse, the dominating role of foreign language teachers and applied linguists has to be acknowledged. It is only recently that content experts have begun participating in this discussion (Ruiz de Zarobe et al., 2011). Breidbach and Viehbrock (2012) provide a good survey of CLIL and recent CLIL research in Germany. Surveys about competence development within the subjects are rare; case studies by Bonnet (2004), Koch and Bründer (2006) or Osterhage (2007) strongly indicate that subject specific competence development is also more sustainable. Despite the promising benefits of CLIL, not every school offers it due to a lack of resources. If schools offer CLIL classes, students are often selected according to their foreign language proficiency, because it is assumed that students with weak language competences are not able to adequately participate and, thus, might disturb CLIL lessons. This selection might lead to the formation of an elite (Breidbach, 2002: 23, Breidbach, 2013: 15). Furthermore, it is simplistic to juxtapose conventional language classes to content and language integrated scenarios, as language classes use content-orientation, too. It is preferable to speak of a continuum of scenarios from focus on form to focus on meaning. Most probably, the balance between the two will vary from model to model, from country to country; maybe, even from school to school and is, to a large extent, dependent on the didactic purpose.

If we acknowledge that the integration of content and additional language learning includes resources from both the target culture(s) and language(s) used across the curriculum, the potential for intercultural and transcultural learning, as demanded in terms of global competences, becomes obvious: due to more language exposure in the target language, more comprehensible language and content input is ultimately provided for the students. This leads to various communication oriented occasions for negotiating language and content meaning via student-student and / or student-teacher interaction. This language interaction in turn produces output that may lead to a desired intake of content and, if applicable, an awareness of cultural idiosyncrasies (Breidbach, Viebrock, 2006: 236). Discourse – in the sense of "language in use, for communication" (Cook, 1989: 6) – in CLIL classrooms is described by Dalton-Puffer (2007), where she claims that the CLIL classroom provides discourse space. The patterns occurring in this discourse space are clearly defined by the institutional school context with role-specific occurrences, such as questions asked by the teacher (Dalton-Puffer, 2007: 123) and language functions, such as defining, explaining, hypothesizing and predicting, which are surprisingly rare (Dalton-Puffer, 2007: 131ff.). Discourse is a means within CLIL settings and a desired end; enabling the learner to share in democratic participation in globalized societies (New London Group, 1996), which is a clearly defined goal of multiliteracies pedagogy. This makes our perception of CLIL by interaction seen in the framework of multiliteracies pedagogy (see chapter 3) more comprehensive.

Figure 1 visualizes these assumptions and hints at their theoretical basis:

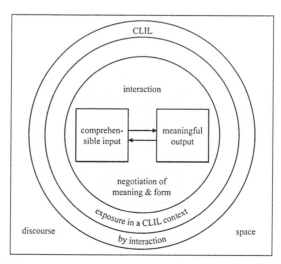

Figure 1: *CLIL by interaction: discourse as a means and an end*

Within a CLIL learning environment, the L2 exposure is evident as the target language is used as a medium to deliver the content and the required language means by comprehensible input (Krashen, 1985). The communicative occasions are initiated by an authentic content topic and corresponding meaningful and relevant tasks for the learners. These tasks lead to interaction within the CLIL classroom through negotiating meaning and form if needed. Because the content and the language input is slightly above the learners' competence the process of negotiating meaning through various forms of interaction takes place by means of discourse (Long, 1983; Gass, 1997; Hall, 2000). During negotiation, meaning output is produced, leading to more L2 exposure. If the output is not comprehensible, it returns to a form of input, which is again above the learner's competence and evokes more interaction to construct meaning by negotiating form, if necessary. Lyster (2007: 57) makes a case for a reactive approach in terms of form-focused instruction. He argues that this kind of "systematic intervention during meaningful interaction" should be combined with a proactive approach to form-focused instruction. This focusing is justified to avoid confusion, which might occur if content- and form-oriented instruction is mixed arbitrarily. He thus propagates a counterbalanced approach (Lyster, 2007, 126).

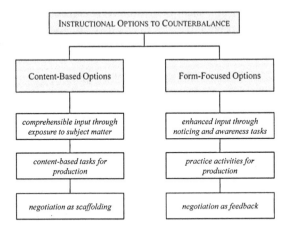

Figure 2:   *Instructional options to counterbalance content-based options and form-focused options (Lyster, 2007: 126)*

This process continues until comprehensible and meaningful output is produced and understood (Swain, 1993, 1995). This process of interaction and negotiation of meaning creates qualitative, quantitative, and genuine learning time of both content and language. As the focus of instruction is on content and language simultaneously, one can speak of an authentic dual learning arrangement.

The notion of counterbalancing content-based and form-focused options will occur throughout the book. As will the concept of *scaffolding*. Gibbons (2002: 10) defines it as

> a special kind of help that assists learners to move toward new skills, concepts, or levels of understanding. Scaffolding is thus the temporary assistance by which a teacher helps a learner know how to do something, so that the learner will later be able to complete a similar task alone.

To put this counterbalanced approach into a global education perspective, it is not enough to consider plurilingual students and perspectives, the content of the subject itself might provide a link to eco-didactics. For that reason CLIL is a promising educational approach, which might lead content teachers to overcome their scepticism and to become active partners in the CLIL business. The preferred pedagogy adapted in this volume is a "multiliteracies" approach (Depuy, 2011, Marenzi, this volume) as the concept is internationally well established and accepted by content teachers, and also because this approach focuses on the need to acquire skills and knowledge in order to cognitively, culturally and socially deal with and create multimodal texts. The major advantage of the literacy concept over competence is seen in its situated social practice. We could claim that competences are essential parts of multiliteracies. As the competence model is used in German curricular and research discourse, we refer to it in the following passages.

Table 1 shows competence dimensions which are inherent to CLIL and indicate that CLIL is more than teaching a subject in an additional language.

Table 1:   CLIL's competence dimensions (translated and modified from Breidbach, 2006: 13)

CLIL's Competence Dimensions	
conceptual	subject specific topics and their terminology
methodological	subject specific methods (e.g. documentation and representation methods)
discursive	subject specific discourses / communication
interactional	social communication skills, learning skills and the ability of being cooperative
reflexive	intercultural approaches

Butzkamm and Caldwell (2009: 41) point out that learning subjects in a foreign language (FL) can be successful in educational contexts that meet the following requirements, with special implications for the use of the mother tongue (MT):

- There is an increased amount of contact time for the foreign language. That means, teaching content subjects through the FL does not replace conventional language classes and systematic language instruction, but is added on. […];
- In order to be able to teach a subject such as biology or geography in an FL, teachers work hard to improve their language skills;
- Teachers must find ways and means to transmit the special MT register of content areas taught in the FL.

These three claims provide a good starting point for raising issues of the language policy involved: Butzkamm and Caldwell's first requirement addresses a misconception of CLIL. In our point of view CLIL is neither a substitution of nor a complement to conventional language teaching. As explained and shown, it is content teaching in a cross-curricular mode (Hoffmann, 2004: 218), possibly supporting plurilingual learners.

The second requirement refers to teacher education. If we underestimate the needs in terms of teacher education, the results could prove fatal:

> […] at its worst, bilingual subject-matter teaching can be inhibitive to both content and language learning, particularly where the teacher lacks the ability to be a simultaneous teacher of language. There is also the danger that immersion schools with a heavy emphasis on fluency at the expense of accuracy produce an error-laden interlanguage (Hammerly, 1998, 1991 in Butzkamm, Caldwell, 2009: 41).

Thus, teacher responsibility and dual qualification can be said to be of concern. In an ideal world every subject teacher is qualified to consider his/her students' language development, not only the language teacher. That is why teachers using the CLIL approach either need to be educated as (foreign) language teachers or must have a high command of the target language as well as a certain awareness of language learning and instruction methods. Policy varies in Europe in this respect. Germany favours a double qualification in both a (foreign) language and a subject. Italy and Greece prefer the subject teachers to teach CLIL, offering on-the-job training (Oddone, 2013: 13ff). The outcome of the reverse responsibility remains to be seen.

Not only should a CLIL teacher possess language skills, they should also be experienced in methodology, especially in the field of specific material design (Mehisto, 2012). This is important because there is a clear lack of appropriate CLIL learning and teaching material. This material must be designed to make an integrative learning of content and language possible. Neither authentic material from the target culture nor translated material from the L1 into the target language can fulfil the premise for dual focused instruction. In consequence, teachers are often left to design their own material.

The third requirement makes us reconsider the role of L1 in a CLIL context. The MT taboo is swept away by Butzkamm and Caldwell (2009) when they claim that we need a paradigm shift in foreign language teaching, which means that the L1 is used systematically as a tool, as it is natural to relate an additional language to what is already there. It remains for us to find out whether this is true for a CLIL context as well. Helbig (2001) and Kollenrott (2007) give empirical evidence that the L1 is not systematically used in CLIL classrooms in Germany. Kollenrott (2007: 248) points out that in her study on 'History taught in English' the learning scenarios are monolingual (target language) and the transfer to L1 is left to the students. Helbig (2001: 319) states that working with texts in the target language does not consider the L1 in a sufficient way, thus ignoring its importance for understanding texts and concepts. Königs supports this view since he believes that bi- / multilingualism should have an instructional permit as a methodological and curricular tool not only to promote the idea of multilingualism, but also to consider the diverse language backgrounds of the students, thus empowering them to express content matters in more than just one language by acquiring bilingual literacy (2013: 34ff.).

To grasp the new quality of CLIL, which is not simply teaching a subject in an additional language, the suitability of various school subjects for a CLIL context should be considered. The critical perspectives of content experts need to be taken into account (Bonnet, Breidbach, 2004). Traditionally, only social science subjects were favoured for the CLIL approach, because they were believed to be more vividly demonstrative with clear connections to the learners' lives in terms of content. Therefore they were assumed to be more suitable for spoken production due to the subjects' inherent descriptive nature. (Sekretariat der Ständigen Konferenz der Kultusminister, 2006: 16f.). According to CLIL's original demand to promote intercultural understanding, it was taken for granted that only social science would meet the premise for such intercultural learning settings due to their affinity to other cultures (Bonnet, 2004: 20; Wegner, 2006: 244). Moreover, social sciences were considered to be cognitively less complex and abstract in comparison to science (ibid.). However, these assumptions have changed with the theories of constructivism as well as through groundbreaking empirical research (Breidbach, 2004), and, meanwhile, the natural sciences are beginning to gain the upper hand on social studies. However, presently all subjects are considered appropriate for CLIL, which goes hand in hand with the paradigm shift from the focus on language instruction within a subject setting to the focus on content itself, where language is being used as a vehicle to communicate content (Wolff, 2013: 18f., Schmelter, 2013: 41). We will use the discourse on teaching history in a CLIL curriculum as an example to articulate one of the major concerns of the proponents of the various subjects, which is related to the fact that CLIL is frequently monolingual and that the gain is linguistic rather than content-oriented.

Hasberg (2004) investigates whether learning history can be achieved in a bilingual history-teaching context. He is positive about the potential of sources from various languages for dealing with the "other". This form of empathy is certainly needed when speaking about the global learner's competences. Hasberg points out, however, that there is a lack of empirical investigation and theoretical foundation on a balanced use of the languages concerned for learning history and their impact on identity formation (2004: 231). Barricceli and Schmieder (2009: 209) discuss the advantages and disadvantages of teaching history in a CLIL setting. They are strictly against a monolingual approach where only the target language is used. They support instead the implementation of scenarios with multilingual resources, if appropriate, where terminology carries culturally loaded meaning. Thus, various languages and their resources could be used as tools to reconstruct not only historical but also cultural realities. This is another way of addressing the MT taboo. A CLIL approach should not only foster one target language, but provide bilingual or multilingual avenues to the content and the concepts where various languages are the tools. In this manner, learner plurilingual competence is supported.

Lyster's counterbalanced approach to CLIL provides a starting point for developing teaching principles, because it combines various instructional practices at the interface of language and content literacy instruction, form-focused instruction as well as decontextualized grammar instruction and incidental focus on language (2007: 25ff.). However, content experts claim that content drives the curriculum (Hasberg, 2004; Barricelli, Schmieder, 2009). If the CLIL approach is to be accepted by the content experts, this priority needs to be accepted. Furthermore, Lyster's model needs to be enhanced by embedding it in a pluri-lingual and global setting (see figure 3).

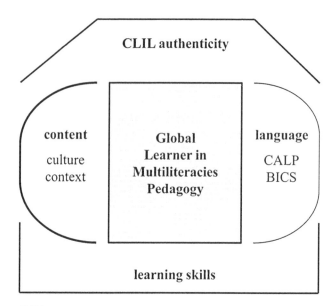

Figure 3:   *CLIL's core principles*

3. Teaching principles seen in the context of a multiliteracies pedagogy

Content-based and form-focused options are essential, but not sufficient for CLIL. The following point of view is quite popular: "Content and Language Integrated Learning (CLIL) is a dual-focused education approach in which an additional language is used for the learning and teaching of both content and language." (Coyle et al., 2010: 1) Coyle elaborates in her 4C's model on the "four contextualized building blocks: content (subject matter), communication (language learning and using), cognition (learning and thinking processes) and culture (developing intercultural understanding and global citizenship)" (ibid. 41). Even though the model considers learning, it must be dealt with more thoroughly. That is why a third dimension, a strong demand for *learning skill* development, must be explicitly stated. Consequently, in addition to content and language, *learning skills* are a third goal for CLIL (Mehisto et al., 2008: 12). CLIL's target aim is to empower learners to deduce content matters with content specific and academic skills through a foreign language by means of discourse and interaction and to deepen comprehension within the foreign language (Königs, 2013: 35f., Breidbach, 2013:16). Furthermore, the dimension of global learning described in chapter 1 has to be added. From these aspects of learning content, language and learning skills some general principles related to CLIL can be deduced. This is of importance as there are no official curricular guidelines for teaching CLIL.

- *Content* drives the curriculum. Content experts claim this priority in terms of curriculum design;
- To communicate the content and negotiate language as well as content meaning, learners must have some basic *interpersonal communicative skills* (BICS), which in turn can also to be seen as a kind of learning skill. The content and the language then may lead to a cognitive *academic linguistic proficiency* (CALP), which is desired for participating within specific content matters (Cummins, 1979). However, BICS must not be underestimated, as this qualification is a prerequisite for any form of communication and discourse, too;
- *Learning skill* development is seen as third goal dimension within the framework of multiliteracies empowering learners to become life-long learners;
- Besides these interwoven core principles with a multiple focus, CLIL instruction offers great potential for *authenticity* in terms of the object (material), the subject (learner) and the situation. (Blell, Kupetz, 2011: 109);
- *Modern media and technologies* provide opportunities for *eLearning and networks* related to CLIL communities which is crucial for dealing with multimodal texts;
- *Scaffolding* is needed when it comes to specific content instruction, which should also focus on context and culture, where applicable. This means that didactic reduction of content, e. g. in terms of simplification, needs to be applied in order to generate essential key concepts, which relate to the learner's existing beliefs or knowledge. Furthermore, *scaffolded* learning is based on Vygotsky's principles of learning in the ZPD;
- CLIL is always subject to active learning, which means that the *amount of learner communication in the target language* must exceed that of the teachers, who is thus a learning facilitator;
- As a *learning facilitator* the teacher needs to deal with language mistakes in a moderate way as the *focus* is clearly *on meaning before accuracy. Feedback* is consequently essential, be it student-student feedback or student-teacher feedback.
- *Learning centeredness and learner centeredness* correspond with a *task-based approach,* which helps students to actively learn content and language simultaneously, without neglecting learning skill development;

- The educational shift from instruction to *construction* goes hand in hand with CLIL, which focuses on learning by construction. Language and content learning needs various approaches that are embedded in specific and general learning skills (e.g. note taking or vocabulary learning as general skills and analyzing graphics or microscope technique as specific skills);
- However, in order to reach the *global learner's competences*, CLIL arrangements must also focus on *multiliteracies* to be developed by an *interaction-oriented approach*.

The CLIL core principle *authenticity* is essential and needs further explanation. It used to be the most outstanding CLIL principle in terms of authentic language usage and content (texts and other materials) coming from the various school subjects. Widdowson (1987) makes a distinction between *genuine* and *authentic* (1978: 80) and describes the process of working with authentic material as *authentication*. We argue that even this is no longer sufficient (Blell, Kupetz, 2011: 109). In terms of learner-orientation, we need to consider the process of authentication which leads us closer to CLIL scenarios considering the subject and the situation as well. Subject orientation – or learner orientation – provides space for a linguistic needs analysis and for the learners' interests. Situation orientation makes it possible to go beyond the classroom. Field trips, excursions and the like come in handy here.

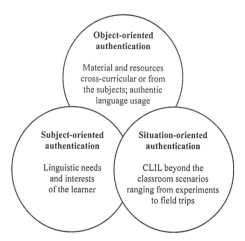

Figure 4:   *Object-, subject- and situation-oriented authentication in CLIL scenarios (Blell, Kupetz, 2011: 109)*

All of these CLIL principles help students in building integrated knowledge and skills for an increasingly interconnected world, which is also the aim of global learning. Multiliteracies pedagogy, on the other hand, tries to grasp the implications of change in our social environment, which leads to an "increasing multiplicity and integration of significant modes of meaning-making, where the textual is also related to the visual, the audio, the spatial, the behavioural, and so on." (New London Group, 1996: 64) Another major issue dealt with by multiliteracies pedagogy is the dichotomy between local diversity and global connectedness. The latter helps to work out the relationship between a multiliteracies pedagogy and a global learning paradigm. Warschauer (1999) elaborates further on the implications of the spread of the Internet for literacy, international language use and additional language learning and teaching. He claims that "we must practise principles of situated learning" with authentic tasks and problem-solving activities to "benefit their (student) future lives as productive citizens" (Warschauer, 1999). CLIL provides genuine discourse space for this.

References

Barricelli, Michele, Schmieder, Ulrich (2009). 'Über Nutzen und Nachteil des bilingualen Sachfachunterrichts. Fremdsprachen- und Geschichtsdidaktik im Dialog', in Daniela Caspari et al. (eds), *Bilingualer Unterricht macht Schule. Beiträge aus der Praxisforschung*. Frankfurt am Main: Peter Lang, pp. 205-20.

Blell, Gabriele, Kupetz, Rita (2011). 'Authentizität und Fremdsprachendidaktik im Dialog', in Wolfgang Funk and Lucia Krämer (eds), *Fiktionen von Wirklichkeit: Authentizität zwischen Materialität und Konstruktion*. Bielefeld: transcript, pp. 99-115.

Bonnet, Andreas (2004). *Chemie im bilingualen Unterricht*. Opladen: Leske und Budrich.

Bonnet, Andreas (2013). 'Unterrichtsprozesse', in Wolfgang Hallet and Frank G. Königs (eds), pp. 187-94.

Bonnet, Andreas, Breidbach, Stephan (eds) (2004). *Didaktiken im Dialog. Konzepte des Lehrens und Wege des Lernens im bilingualen Sachfachunterricht*. Frankfurt am Main: Peter Lang.

Breidbach, Stephan (2002). 'Bilingualer Sachfachunterricht als neues interdisziplinäres Forschungsfeld', in Stephan Breidbach et al. (eds), pp. 11-30.

Breidbach, Stephan (2006). 'Was hat das Denken mit Sprechen zu tun?', *Praxis Fremdsprachenunterricht* 3: 10-5.

Breidbach, Stefan (2013). 'Geschichte und Entstehung des Bilingualen Unterrichts in Deutschland', in Wolfgang Hallet and Frank G. Königs (eds), 18-26.

Breidbach, Stephan et al. (eds) (2002). *Bilingualer Sachfachunterrich. Didaktik, Lehrer-/Lernerforschung und Bildungspolitik zwischen Theorie und Empirie.* Frankfurt am Main: Peter Lang.

Breidbach, Stephan, Viebrock, Britta (2006). 'Bilingualer Sachfachunterricht aus Sicht wissenschaftlicher und praktischer Theoretiker', in Wolfgang Gehring (ed.), *Fremdsprachenunterricht heute.* Oldenburg: Oldenburger Forum Fremdsprachendidaktik, pp. 234-56.

Breidbach, Stephan, Viehbrock, Britta (2012). 'CLIL in Germany – results from recent research in a contested field of education', *International CLIL Research Journal* 1, 4: 5-16.

Butzkamm, Wolfgang, Caldwell, John A. W. (2009). *The Bilingual Reform: A paradigm shift in foreign language teaching.* Tübingen: Narr.

Cook, Guy (1989). *Discourse.* Oxford: Oxford University Press.

Coyle, Do et al. (eds) (2010). *CLIL – Content and Language Integrated Learning.* Cambridge: Cambridge University Press.

Dalton-Puffer, Christiane (2007). *Discourse in Content and Language Integrated Learning (CLIL) Classrooms.* Amsterdam: John Benjamins.

Depuy, Beatrice (2011). 'CLIL: Achieving its goals through a multiliteracies framework', *Latin American Journal of Content & Language Integrated Learning* 4, 2: 21-32.

Gass, M. Susan (1997). *Input, Interaction and the Second Language Learner.* Mahwah, NJ: Lawrence Erlbaum Associates.

Hall, Joan et al. (eds) (2000). *Second and Foreign Language Learning through Classroom Interaction.* Mahwah, NJ: Lawrence Erlbaum Associates.

Hallet, Wolfgang (2005). 'Bilingualer Unterricht: Fremdsprachig denken, lernen und handeln', *Der Fremdsprachliche Unterricht Englisch* 78: 2-8.

Hallet, Wolfgang (2013). 'Bilingualer Unterricht als Aufgabe der Schulentwicklung', in Wolfgang Hallet and Frank G. Königs (eds), 52-9.

Hallet, Wolfgang (2013). 'Geschichte und Entstehung des Bilingualen Unterrichts in Deutschland: Bilingualer Unterricht und Gesellschaftspolitik', in Wolfgang Hallet and Frank G. Königs (eds), 11-17.

Hallet, Wolfgang, Königs, Frank G. (eds) (2013). *Handbuch Bilingualer Unterricht. Content and Language Integrated Learning.* Seelze: Klett & Kallmeyer.

Hasberg, Wolfgang (2004). 'Historisches Lernen im bilingualen Geschichtsunterricht (?)', in Andreas Bonnet and Stephan Breidbach (eds), pp. 221-36.

Helbig, Beate (2001). *Das bilinguale Sachfach Geschichte. Eine empirische Studie zur Arbeit mit französischsprachigen (Quellen-)Texten.* Tübingen: Stauffenburg.

Hoffmann, Reinhard (2004). 'Geographie als bilinguales Sachfach', in Andreas Bonnet and Stephan Breidbach (eds), pp. 207-19.

Koch, Angela, Bründer, Wolfgang (2006). 'Fachbezogener Wissenserwerb im bilingualen naturwissenschaftlichen Anfangsunterricht', *Zeitschrift für Didaktik der Naturwissenschaften* 12: 67-76.

Königs, Frank G. (2013). 'Sprachen, Sprachenpolitik und Bilingualer Unterricht', in Wolfgang Hallet and Frank G. Königs (eds), pp. 46-52.

Kollenrott, Anne I. (2007). *Sichtweisen auf deutsch-englischen bilingualen Geschichtsunterricht.* Frankfurt am Main: Peter Lang.

Krashen, Stephen D. (1985). *The Input Hypothesis: Issues and implications.* New York: Longman.

Leisen, Josef (2005). 'Wechsel der Darstellungsformen. Ein Unterrichtsprinzip für alle Fächer', *Der Fremdsprachliche Unterricht* 78: 9-11.

Lyster, Roy (2007). *Learning and Teaching Languages through Content. A counterbalanced approach.* Amsterdam: John Benjamins.

Marsh, David (2002). *CLIL/EMILE. The European Dimension. Actions, trends and foresight potential.* Public Services Contract DG EAC: European Commission. Jyväskylä, Finland: UniCOM, Continuing Education Centre, University of Jyväskylä, pp. 65-88.

Mehisto, Peeter et al. (2008). *Uncovering CLIL. Content and language integrated learning in bilingual and multilingual education.* Oxford: Maxmillan.

Mehisto, Peeter (2012). 'Criteria for producing CLIL learning material', *Encuentro* 21: 15-33.

New London Group (1996). 'A pedagogy of multiliteracies: designing social futures', *Harvard Educational Review* 66, 1: 60-92. 01 November 2013, retrieved from <http://her.hepg.org/content/17370n67v22j160u/?p=21a6d6e53104451c8 2f133aefdd176e7&pi=2>

Nold, Günter et al. (2008). 'Klassen mit bilingualem Sachfachunterricht: Englisch als Arbeitssprache', in DESI-Konsortium (eds), *Unterricht und Kompetenzerwerb in Deutsch und Englisch: Ergebnisse der DESI-Studie.* Weinheim: Beltz Verlag, pp. 451-57.

O'Loughlin, Eddie, Wegimont, Liam (eds) (2002). *Global Education in Europe to 2015: Strategy, policies, and perspectives – outcomes and papers of the Europe-wide global education congress Maastricht, The Netherlands 15th-17th November 2002.* 01 November 2013, retrieved from

<http://www.coe.int/t/dg4/nscentre/Resources/Publications/GE_Maastrich t_Nov2002.pdf>

Oddone, Cristina (2013). *Web 2.0 and CLIL. Task and material design to scaffold learning in interactive environments.* Unpublished dissertation thesis. University of Genova.

Osterhage, Sven (2007). 'Sachfachkönnen (scientific literacy) bilingual und monolingual unterrichteter Biologieschüler: Ein Kompetenzvergleich', in Daniela Caspari et al. (eds), *Bilingualer Unterricht macht Schule: Beiträge aus der Praxisforschung.* Frankfurt am Main: Peter Lang, pp. 41-50.

Ruiz de Zarobe, Yolanda et al. (2011). 'Introduction – Content and Foreign Language Integrated Learning: A plurilingual perspective', in Yolanda Ruiz de Zarobe et al. (eds), pp. 11-7.

Ruiz de Zarobe, Yolanda et al. (eds) (2011). *Content and Foreign Language Integrated Learning. Contributions to multilingualism in European contexts.* Bern: Peter Lang.

Rymarczyk, Jutta, Bongartz, Christiane M. (2010). '40 Jahre Bilingualer Sachfachunterricht in Deutschland: Versuch einer Standortbestimmung', in Christiane Bongartz and Jutta Rymarczyk (eds). *Languages Across the Curriculum. Ein multiperspektivischer Zugang.* Frankfurt am Main: Peter Lang, pp.7-23.

Schmelter, Lars (2013). 'Entwicklungstendenzen und Desiderata der bilingualen Sachfachdidaktik', in Wolfgang Hallet and Frank G. Königs (eds), pp. 40-5.

Sekretariat der Ständigen Konferenz der Kultusminister der Länder der Bundesrepublik Deutschlang (eds) (2006). *Konzepte für den bilingualen Unterricht – Erfahrungsberichte und Vorschläge zur Weiterentwicklung.* Kultusminister Konferenz. 01 November 2013, retrieved from <http://www.kmk.org/fileadmin/veroeffentlichungen_beschluesse/2006/2 006_04_10-Konzepte-bilingualer-Unterricht.pdf>

Swain, Merrill (1993). 'The output hypothesis. Just speaking and writing aren't enough', *The Canadian Modern Languages Review* 50, 1: 158-64.

Swain, Merrill, Lapkin, Sharon (1995). 'Problems in output and the cognitive processes they Generate: a step towards second language learning', *Applied Linguistics* 16, 3: 371-91.

Swain, Merill, Lapkin, Sharon (2006). 'Multilingualism through immersion education?', in Dieter Wolff (ed.), *Mehrsprachige Individuen – vielsprachige Gesellschaften.* Frankfurt am Main: Peter Lang, pp. 31-45.

Vollmer, Helmut J. (2006). *Language across the Curriculum.* Strasbourg: Language Policy Division, Council of Europe, pp. 1-12.

Vollmer, Helmut J. (2013). 'Das Verhältnis von Sprach- und Inhaltslernen im Bilingualen Unterricht', in Wolfgang Hallet and Frank G. Königs (eds), pp. 124-31.

Wegner, Anke (2006). 'Bilinguales Lehren und Lernen im Spannungsfeld von politischer und didaktischer Reflexion', in Sabine Doff and Anke Wegner (eds), *Fremdsprachendidaktik im 20. Jahrhundert. Konstituierung einer wissenschaftlichen Disziplin im Spannungsfeld von Theorie und Praxis.* München: Langenscheidt, pp. 243-61.

Warschauer, Mark (1999). 'Millennialism and media: language, literacy, and technology in the 21st century', *AILA Review* 14: 49-59. 01 November 2013, retrieved from http://www.aila.info/download/publications/review/AILA14.pdf#page=55.

Wesche, Marjorie B. (2002). 'Early French immersion: how has the original Canadian model stood the test of time?', in Petra Burmeister et al. (eds), *An Integrated View of Language Development: Papers in honour of Henning Wode.* Trier: Wissenschaftlicher Verlag Trier, pp. 357-75.

Wildhage, Manfred, Otte, Edgar (eds) (2003). *Praxis des bilingualen Unterrichts.* Berlin: Cornelsen.

Wolff, Dieter (2000).'Möglichkeiten zur Entwicklung von Mehrsprachigkeit in Europa', in Gerhard Bach and Susanne Niemeier (eds). *Bilingualer Unterricht. Grundlagen, Methoden, Praxis, Perspektiven.* Frankfurt am Main: Peter Lang, pp. 159-72.

Wolff, Dieter (2013). 'CLIL als europäisches Konzept.' in Wolfgang Hallet and Frank G. Königs (eds), pp. 18-26.

Peer-to-peer scaffolding in a primary school science class

Carmen Becker, Leibniz Universität Hannover, Germany

1. CLIL in science at primary level

Science seems to be the most favoured subject for teaching content matter through a foreign language at primary level in Germany (Burmeister, Ewig, 2010: 100). The specific German primary level subject *Sachunterricht* "comprises various areas within the natural and social sciences" (Burmeister, Ewig, 2010: 100) such as Biology, History and Geography. According to Burmeister and Ewig (2010: 100) the popularity of science for CLIL stems from the direct nature of the "comprehensible contexts" that can be dealt with.

Burmeister and Massler (2010: 7) see CLIL at primary level as a superordinate concept, which covers a continuum of two extremes. On the one hand, there are programmes that offer CLIL modules, where, for example, science subject matter is only sporadically taught in the foreign language. On the other hand, there are immersion programmes whose main characteristics are that a substantial part of the instruction in the different subjects is done in English throughout the whole duration of primary education.

> In order to allow in-depth learning of complex science subject-matter in CLIL, the teacher needs to create a learning environment which actively involves the students. [...] The CLIL teacher has to ensure that the children can understand the content at all times (Burmeister, Ewig, 2010: 104).

Furthermore, Burmeister and Ewig stress the importance of interaction between teachers and learners and especially focus on scaffolding to make both content and language accessible to primary students (Burmeister, Ewig, 2010: 105). This is also emphasized by Böttger (2013: 70) who claims that the use of a great variety of scaffolding techniques by the teacher is necessary in order to ensure positive long-term effects for language and subject matter learning at primary level. Therefore the question arises as to whether there is also potential in peer-to-peer interaction in the German primary CLIL context within the framework of sociocultural theory, in order to further develop competences in the language and at the level of the conceptual understanding of the content.

2. Socio-cultural theory

2.1 The Zone of Proximal Development

According to socio-cultural theory, learning is a process that is highly social and based on the interaction between individuals. Vygotsky, whose works mainly laid the foundation for socio-cultural theory, argued that the basis of the development of an individual's higher mental functions is formed by "internalized social relationships" (Vygotsky, 1981: 74).

> Every function in the child's cultural development appears twice: first on the social level and later, on the individual level; first between people (*interpsychological*), and then *inside* the child (*intrapsychological*). This applies equally to all voluntary attention, to logical memory, and to the formation of concepts. All the higher mental functions originate as actual relations between people (Vygotsky, 1978: 57).

As Shrum and Glissan (2005: 19) sum up, "In Vygotsky's [...] view [...] learning precedes and contributes to development, and the learner's language performance with others exceeds what the learner is able to do alone". Vygotsky (1978: 86) described this developmental process of expanding the learners' current level using the metaphor of the zone of proximal development (ZPD), which he defines in this manner:

> It is the distance between the actual developmental level as determined by independent problem-solving and the level of potential development as determined through problem-solving under adult guidance or in collaboration with more capable peers.

2.2 Scaffolding

Tasks that students can confidently carry out on their own without any assistance lie within the area of self-regulation (van Lier, 1996: 190). Beyond this area lies a "range of knowledge and skills which the person can only access with someone's assistance" (van Lier, 1996: 190). This assistance can be given by linking a new challenging complex action to pre-existing knowledge or previously acquired competences. According to van Lier "This material, which one might say is within reach, constitutes the ZPD" (van Lier, 1996: 190 f). Anything that lies outside the ZPD is not yet accessible for learning.

Little et al. (2007: 24) emphasise that the "Development in the ZPD [...] proceeds from other-regulation to self-regulation, towards increasing autonomy". They further stress that in classrooms the teacher's major function is to foster this development "but it can also be mediated by interaction with more capable peers" (Little et. al, 2007: 24). This has also been underlined by van

Lier (1996) who points out that besides inner resources, peer interactions at different levels play an important role in expanding the ZPD:

- assistance from more capable peers or adults
- interaction with equal peers
- interaction with less capable peers (in accordance with the Roman dictum *Docende discimus* – (we learn by teaching)
- inner resources (van Lier, 1996: 193).

The interaction process of assisting learners in extending their area of self-regulation and moving them through the ZPD by providing assistance in a problem-solving task was defined by the developmental psychologist Bruner (1983: 60) using the metaphor of scaffolding.

> A process of setting up the situation to make a child's entry easy and successful and then gradually pulling back and handing the role to the child as he becomes skilled enough to manage it (...) one sets the game, provides a scaffold to assure that the child's ineptitudes can be rescued or rectified by appropriate interventions, and then removes the scaffold part by part as the reciprocal structure can stand on its own.

Other researchers followed Bruner's concept of scaffolding and describe it similarly. Maybin, Mercer, and Stierer (1992: 186), for example, see scaffolding as "[...] temporary, but essential [...]" to support learners' learning through interaction. Brown and Palincsar (1989: 122) depict scaffolding as "[...] the idea of an adjustable and temporary support that can be removed when no longer necessary". Whatever definition suits best, scaffolding should not be confused with the term "help". As Gibbons (2002: 10) notes, scaffolding aims at assisting students to enable them "[...] to move toward new skills, concepts, or levels of understanding".

Many different types of expert-novice interactions that foster transformation in the ZPD through scaffolding have been identified. Table 1 (Lidz, 1991: 6) gives an overview of twelve scaffolding interactions, as they occur in reciprocal action between novices and experts such as parents or other caretakers and children:

Table 1:   Twelve component behaviours of adult mediating instructions (Lidz, 1991: 6)

1. Intentionality	Attempt to consciously influence the actions of child. Including: efforts to keep interaction going, engage child's attention, maintain goal orientation.
2. Meaning	Help child's understanding: highlight important facts, mark differences, offer related information.

3. Transcendence	Promote associations to related experiences in the past, project child into future.
4. Joint regard	Use personal pronoun "we" to talk about experiences, see experience through the eyes of the child.
5. Sharing of experiences	Tell child about own experiences.
6. Task regulation	Facilitate problem-solving, give a principle of solution, discuss strategic thinking.
7. Praise/ Encouragement	Verbal and non-verbal communication with child when child has done something good, keep its self-esteem high.
8. Challenge	Activities take place in the ZPD of child, challenge child beyond actual developmental level but not further.
9. Psychological differentiation	It is the child's task, not the mediator's. Goal is to ensure a learning experience for child.
10. Contingent responsivity	Ability to read child's behaviour and to respond to it.
11. Affective involvement	Give child a sense of caring and enjoyment in doing the task.
12. Change	Communicate improvements and changes in the child to child.

Since scaffolding also occurs in classrooms between teachers as experts and students as novices, different researchers have identified various verbal scaffolding techniques (Thürmann, 2013: 238). According to Massler and Ioannou-Georgiou (2010: 63) there are two main categories, which characterize scaffolding in student-teacher interaction:

- input-oriented scaffolding techniques which focus on making teacher L2 input understandable for students; and
- output-oriented scaffolding techniques which focus on how students can be assisted in expressing understanding and in participating actively in a CLIL lesson, even with limited L2 competence.

The following scaffolding technique, as used by a teacher in a Northern German English-as-a-foreign-language classroom, was observed by Gerngross in 2007. Here, the teacher scaffolds the student's output by recasting and rephrasing to fill in the right lexical items. At the end of the exchange the student finally includes the new lexical item in his/her active repertoire.

S: My mother is krank.
T: Oh, really? Your mother is ill. I'm sorry to hear that. What's the problem?
S: Have got Grippe.

T:	Oh, she's got the flu.
S:	Yes, big Kopfschmerzen.
T:	Ah, she's got a bad headache.
S:	She's got a bad headache. Yes.

(personal information from Gerngross 2007)

2.3   Peer-scaffolding

But not only expert-novice scaffolding at the level of adults interacting with children plays an important role. As pointed out by Vygotsky (1978) and van Lier (1996) peer interaction at the level of children and older students working together collaboratively is also regarded as an important factor in ZPD work. However, as Li pointed out, one has to take into account that, even though scaffolding occurs among peers, they might "[...] not always produce accurate forms in their talk" (Li, 2009: 24) as adult experts do.

To foster peer-peer interaction and scaffolding in the classroom, teachers have to consider engaging learners in communicative collaborative tasks, which demand that students actively work towards a common goal and negotiate meaning by interacting in groups. This is stressed by Gibbons (2010) who underlines that "Students' cooperation with other students increases, and so is (sic) their output. They actively contribute to their learning of the language, because they try to make the meaning of their utterances clear for the whole group" (Gibbons, 2010: 8).

3.   The dinosaur project

3.1   The research question

Since peer-to-peer scaffolding seems to be a very powerful means to foster the expansion of the ZPD and has been proved to occur naturally in classroom interaction among adolescents or adult learners in several studies (Donato, 1994; Gallimore, Tharp, 1990; Wood, Bruner, Ross, 1976; Li, 2009), the main goal of the research project was to find out a) whether this type of scaffolding occurs in collaborative group work interactions among children at primary level, b) which peer-scaffolding techniques are used and c) at what level they occur?

3.2   The participants, teacher, and materials

The participants of the project were 26 students (14 boys and 12 girls) of a 4th grade in a primary science class aged 9-10. The class is an English total immersion class within a regular German primary school. All subjects were taught in English from grade one on.

The class teacher is a non-native speaker who was trained as a teacher for EFL and has neither specific training to teach an immersive class nor any specific training to teach science.

Due to very limited funding, the school has no access to authentic resources. The students mainly use German science books and materials which the teacher develops on the basis of websites. For the research project, authentic English science books were supplied for the first time.

3.3   The task of the Dinosaur Project

After having studied dinosaurs for a period of four weeks in the regular science class, the students had to cooperatively plan, develop and make posters about dinosaurs and present them at the end of the session. The students worked in groups of four to five. Each group assigned an English guard, whose responsibility it was to remind all members to use the target language and a time guard, who had to keep track of the time. Also each group focused on different types of dinosaurs, which were drawn by lot at the beginning of the lesson. All groups were asked to gather identical kinds of information on the dinosaurs, which included the meaning of the name, the size and weight as well as the food it ate, information on defence behaviour and additional information, such as striking characteristics of its body or behaviour.

In order to ensure as much reciprocal peer-to-peer interaction as possible, by restricting the number of participants in individual tasks, each group then split into two teams; Team One was asked to investigate the name, size etc. whereas Team Two researched defence behaviour and additional information.

To obtain all the information needed, the students used scientific books in the target language, folders with special information which had been taken from a website, folders with cut-outs as well a computer with Internet access. The teacher estimated a period of twenty minutes for the first task. Following the first part of their investigation, both teams were asked to exchange their findings in order to have a common ground for the following tasks and also to foster the discussion among peers and peer-to-peer interaction. The fourth task included planning and preparing the poster within a time frame of twenty minutes. The teacher offered a large poster for each group, as well as several small ones. Additionally, the group had to decide who would present which piece of information.

3.4   Data collection and analysis

Two researchers collected classroom interactive data during one whole working period of 90 minutes from the beginning to the end. Following the introduction and instruction phase of the teacher, various groups were videotaped during their collaborative group work sessions, as well as during the final presentation. Both researchers started filming the interaction as soon as the students began working on their tasks. They both did not interfere in the discussion of the students. So the study focused on the interaction that took place among peers in the classroom.

The data was transcribed according to GAT 2 conventions (Selting et al., 2009) by Haasler (2011) as part of her Bachelor thesis at the Leibniz Universität Hannover and analysed in two steps. First, all instances of scaffolding episodes were identified. Secondly, the data was coded and finally quantified. All names were anonymised and pseudonyms used in the transcriptions. The identification of the scaffolding instances was based on seven types of peer-to-peer scaffolding categories compiled by Li (2009) analysing data from various earlier sources such as Donato, 1994, Gallimore and Tharp, 1990 and Wood, Bruner and Ross, 1976, which she applied to her own study, investigating peer-to-peer scaffolding of fifteen Chinese EFL learners at university level who had been studying English between thirteen to sixteen years. The task the learners were involved in focused on grammar. The learners had to rewrite an essay by changing certain marked phrases into relative clauses. To master the task they had to work in groups of three to four students negotiating the use of the right forms.

Table 2:   Seven possible kinds of scaffolding in peer-peer interactions (Li, 2009: 18)

Recruitment (R)	The learners' attention and interest in the task is recruited.
Simplifying the task (S)	The requirements of the task are reduced, by taking one step at a time to solve the problem.
Direction Maintenance (DM)	Uphold the purpose of the goal.
Marking Critical Features (MCF)	Compare what has been offered as solution with the optimal solution.

Frustration Control (FC)	Frustration can arise during the solving process and should be controlled.
Demonstration (D)	An optimal solution of the problem is demonstrated.
Feedback (F)	Give feedback on the performance of the learners.

Haasler (2011) reviewed the video recordings three times in order to verify the coding and the quantifications. She and an additional evaluator reached 92 % agreement on all identified scaffolding functions. In the case of discrepancy, co-operative reviewing of the recordings and discussion of the definitions resolved the disagreements.

3.5   Quantity of Scaffolding Categories

As revealed by the analyzed data, some types of scaffolding are predominant. The following table illustrates the occurrences in numbers.

Table 3:   Quantity of the scaffolding categories (Haasler, 2011: 25)

N= 114	Occurrence	Occurrence in %
Recruitment (R)	12	11.5
Simplifying the Task (S)	7	6.7
Direction Maintenance (DM)	7	6.7
Marking Critical Features (MCF)	0	0
Frustration Control (FC)	3	2.9
Demonstration (D)	7	6.7
Feedback (F)	54	51.9
Managing (M)	10	9.6
Supplementing (SU)	4	3.8

The main difference between the scaffolding categories compiled by Li in table 2 and the ones found by Haasler (2011) in table 3 is that two additional scaffolding types were added after analysing the data: Managing and Supplementing. The two extra categories were added because they were not identified by Li (2009) but occurred in the data.

According to Haasler (2011: 25)

> Managing takes place when a student gives instructions and acts like a manager/tutor, i.e. telling another student what s/he can or cannot do. Supplementing, on the other hand, occurs, whenever one student finishes the thought of someone else, probably because a word has been forgotten or they do not remember what they wanted to say.

The data compiled by Haasler (2011) reveals that Feedback is the predominant kind of scaffolding in the primary school science class. It made up 51.9 % of all recorded scaffolding interactions, followed by Recruitment (11.5 %) and Managing (9.6 %). However, the gap between the occurring percentages is great. According to Haasler (2011: 25) "None of the other scaffolding categories – Simplifying, Direction Maintenance, Demonstration, Frustration Control, and Supplementing – reach seven percent in descending order". The Marking of Critical Features was not noticed at all in the primary school students' interaction.

3.6 Feedback

The most significant peer-to-peer scaffolding category found in the data is, as in Li's study (2009), Feedback. It was possible to identify it in almost every second sentence. The primary students provide and receive Feedback for praising their peers' work, for expressing agreement or disagreement, or for expressing attentiveness (Haasler, 2011: 26).

Positive Feedback

Here, Henrik is praised for the picture he cut out.

```
37   Monica:   <<to katrin> cut it out aber
                                       but
               very very neatly>
38   Katrin:   yes                           (F)
39   Henrik:   so::::? <<shows a picture he cut out>
               (D)
               like this>
40   Julius:   wo:::w (.) really good        (F)
41   Monica:   hm=hm                         (F)
```

Expressing Agreement

Here, Sandra needs a piece of paper.

```
57   Sandra:   give me a paper              (R)
58   Niko:     i give you a paper           (F)
```

Expressing Disagreement

Here, Ina does not agree with the spot Kai has chosen for a picture on the poster.

```
26   Kai:     okay here this <<looks for spot on poster for his
              picture> i oh:where >        (R)
27   Ina:     ne: uhm du                   (F)
              nope    you
28   Tim:     yes i:                       (F)
29   Ina:     no:                          (F)
```

Expressing Attentiveness

Here, Ben signals to Tom that he listened to what Tom said.

```
01   Tom:     konnte: with the tai:l a bone
              could
              of the tyrannossaur rex (.) break
02   Ben:     aha okay                     (F)
```

Although different kinds of Feedback occur in the data, the students' spoken interactions are usually not improved and there is no evidence for progress in linguistic or communicative competence. Most of the time, the students give feedback in the form of limited one-word "yes" and "no" answers but there is no evidence for the occurrence of a justification for likes and dislikes of certain aspects or more detailed explanation in the Feedback (Haasler, 2011: 26)

Moreover, there is also evidence for incorrect Feedback, as in the following example, where Mona wants to write down the word "period". Lisa reads the word and stresses its syllables, pronouncing it correctly (line 53). Mona does not approve of Lisa's pronunciation and repeats the word using the pronunciation she thinks is right (line 54). Even though she knows the correct form, Lisa agrees with Mona's wrong pronunciation and repeats it, claiming that she knew this was the correct pronunciation from the start (line 55). Next, Mona repeats the word stressing syllables twice, while she is writing it on the cardboard (line 56). So, in the end, Mona convinced Lisa that she used an improper pronunciation of "period" and both girls use the form incorrectly (Haasler, 2011: 21).

Wrong Correction

```
53   Lisa:    <<reads> period>
54   Mona:    PÄriod
55   Lisa:    ja ich weiß (.) PÄriod
              yes I know
56   Mona:    <<writing on poster> pä-ri-od (.) pä-ri-od >
```

In her study, Li (2009: 31) discovered that feedback on peer performance is not as productive as that of the teachers, because "[...] the students lack the practice or opportunities to handle discourse and stimulate other peers' thinking by asking questions as the teacher does". Since Li's study was based on the interaction of university students, giving detailed feedback would therefore be virtually impossible for primary school students. However, there are also positive aspects of the limited feedback. Analysing the data, Haasler (2011: 26) observed that:

> Positive feedback enriches the atmosphere of group work situations, so that the motivation is maintained. Feedback is also needed to reach consensus in the group and to make sure one's work and oneself are not ignored, but a complete member of the group. (…) the language which students use to give feedback is not as important as the fact that they provide feedback. The received feedback will improve on the language base, as the students themselves reach higher levels of proficiency. Until then, it is important to provide group members with feedback to the best of the individuals' abilities.

3.7   Recruitment

The next expressed type of scaffolding, although with an enormous distance to Feedback, is Recruitment (11.5%). In comparison to Feedback, it is used in the context of one topic – to get someone else to listen to one's own questions (Haasler, 2011: 27).

Recruiting interest to receive help

Here, Dana needs Sarah's help to spell the word "one" correctly.

```
63   Dana:    sara? sara?
              wie wird ONe geschrieben?  (R)
              how do you spell
64   Sara:    WAnn?                      (F)
              when
65   Dana:    ONe                        (S)
```

Here, Bastian wants to know the meaning of unknown words.

```
01   Bastian: <<reading> this skeleton was
              described by plantologists>        (-) <<f>
              but > i don`t know what this means (.) in the
              text florian              (R)
02   Florian: what?
03   Bastian: this here <<shows florian     text>>
04   Florian: u::hm
05   Bastian: this and this
06   Florian: uhm this is the name of the plantologist
              (D)
```

Recruiting for reassurance

Here, Anna needs to know if she has the right information at her disposal.

```
05   Anna:    <<f> wie viele tonnen > wiegt der noch mal (.) fünf
              to sechs ne? (R)
              how many tons does it weigh again five to six right
```

Recruiting for finding something to do

Here, Tim wants to participate in the work of his group, but does not know what he should be doing.

```
01   Tim:     i had asked you something (.) what we (.) can DO
              now
```

As can be seen in the examples, Recruitment is a useful means for receiving positive or negative feedback or information on the content or task. The data implies that students can achieve more with the help of their peer-group than working individually. Recruitment helps to build up the content knowledge of the group. In two out of the three examples the students used code-switching to recruit assistance regarding the content. However, code-switching can be seen as a supporting factor for scaffolding the understanding of the content (Haasler, 2011: 28).

3.8   Managing

Managing reaches a percentage of 9.6, and is the last of the three most dominant scaffolding types in the Dinosaur Project. Even though it does not occur as often as Recruitment or Feedback, it seems to play a major role in creating and keeping a positive atmosphere in the group (Haasler, 2011: 28).

Managing because being asked

Here, Tina directly asks her group for a task she can do.

```
13   Tina:    what do i have to do?        (R)
14   Mona:    yes u[hm                     (F)
15   Lisa:        [yes                     (F)
16   Anna:    genau uhm <<excited>> if uhm
              exactly
              you can uhm you uhm you can
              uhm > ta::ke my uhm [my folder and uhm (---) uhm
              (M)/(F)
17   Bibi:                        [du kannst schreiben (.) du
              kannst aufschreiben wie schwer der is
                            (SU)/(M)
              you can write you can write about how heavy it is
```

```
18   Anna:    and uhm look for informations about the u:hm and
              the type of
              schreib auf wie schwer
              der is wenn du was zu tun willst
              (M)
              write about how heavy it is if you want to do some-
              thing
```

Managing without being asked

Here, Monica assigns a task without being explicitly asked to do so.

```
33   Katrin:  sonst find ich nichts mehr über die zähne v[om
              I don't find anything about the teeth
34   Julius:                                     [hm=hm  (F)
35   Monica:  du sollst das jetzt schön ausschn[eiden
              (M)
              you are supposed to cut it out neatly
```

In Li's study, Managing is not taken into consideration as a scaffolding category in peer interaction. However, it seems to be important at primary level. The data reveals that some students take the role of a manager in their group. Their function is to ensure that all group members actively engage in the tasks. The data also reveals that the manager independently took over this role without being asked by their teacher. They guarantee that no participant feels left out and that all group members stay on task. They organise the work by structuring the content and task (Haasler, 2011: 28).

4. Conclusion

The research project reveals that peer-to-peer scaffolding generally occurs during collaborative group work tasks at primary level. However, many peer-peer scaffolding types like Marking Critical Features or Frustration Control identified by Li (2009) do not occur at all, whereas Feedback occurs most (Haasler, 2011: 29).

Nevertheless, the data shows that scaffolding occurs among peers in order to assist each other in fulfilling the task of creating a poster with the information required. It can be observed that the students focus less on form or content, they focus on negotiating meaning and involving all participants in their work. Sometimes they get lost in organizational problems, i.e. deciding how to design the poster, or finding a pair of scissors to cut out a picture. As a consequence, they do not always work in a goal-oriented way.

Feedback, Recruitment and Managing help the students to assist each other carrying out the task, but according to Haasler (2011: 30) "[...] it is questionable whether the assistance helped the others to perform in their potential Zone of Proximal Development" at the level of mastery of a conceptual understanding of the content matter or communicative and linguistic competence.

There seems to be evidence in the data that students at primary level need the help of a teacher or a more capable peer to perform in their ZPD, since very few peer-to-peer interactions in which students assisted each other in their language performance occurred as exemplified by the spelling incident, in which Sara assisted Dana in the spelling of the word 'one'. However, the data implies that the students in the specific classroom context did not generally succeed in moving beyond the level of their current development thanks to the assistance of equally able or less capable peers, for these also generally lack the competence of giving tutor-like feedback on linguistic performance or content (Haasler, 2011: 29). The data therefore does not show that students at primary level expand their ZPD by interacting "with less capable peers (in accordance with the Roman dictum *Docende discimus* – (we learn by teaching)" as stated by van Lier (1996: 193). Reasons for this could lie in the only rudimentarily developed intercessional competences of the young learners which according to Bonnet (2013: 192) are crucial for subject matter and content learning in collaborative learning environments.

Finally and most importantly, the data also confirms that the development of the ZPD in the specific classroom context of the research project occurs mainly at a managerial level. Despite the fact that the primary students share a beginners' level of competence at which interaction in the mother tongue is natural, they are capable of assisting each other in order to successfully carry out the task and reach their goal, using fairly high amounts of utterances in the L2. The data therefore implies that scaffolding at managerial level is an important interaction category, playing a significant role in the young CLIL learners' classrooms. In the long run, scaffolding at managerial level could therefore serve as a springboard for different types of scaffolding and could lead to an increase of reciprocal interaction regarding subject matter and language. Further research needs to be carried out in order to investigate whether peer-to-peer scaffolding which furthers the development of the ZPD at the linguistic or content matter level could be supported by interaction on a managerial level and by systematically developing the interactional competences of the learners.

References

Burmeister, Petra, Ewig, Michel (2011). 'Integrating science and foreign language learning', in Ute Massler and Petra Burmeister (eds), pp.100-06.

Bonnet, Andreas (2013). 'Unterrichtsprozesse: Interaktion und Bedeutungsaushandlung', in Wolfgang Hallet and Frank G. Königs (eds), pp.187-94.

Böttger, Heiner (2013). 'Bilingualer Unterricht in Primarschulen: Die Fremdsprache in den Lernbereichen der Grundschule', in Wolfgang Hallet and Frank G. Königs (eds), pp. 60-66.

Brown, Ann, Palincsar, Annemarie (1989). 'Guided, cooperative learning and individual knowledge acquisition', in Lauren B. Resnick (ed.), *Knowing, Learning and Instruction: Essays in honor of Robert Glaser*. Hillsdale, NJ: Lawrence Erlbaum, pp. 393-451

Bruner, Jerome S. (1983). *Child's Talk: Learning to use language*. New York: Vintage Books.

Donato, Richard (1994). 'Collective scaffolding in second language learning', in James P. Lantolf and Gabriela Appel (eds), *Vygotskyan Approaches to Second Language Learning Research*. Norwood, NJ: Ablex, pp. 33-56

Gallimore, Ronald, Tharp, Roland G. (1990). 'Teaching mind in society: teaching, schooling, and literate discourse', in Luis C. Moll (ed.), *Vygotsky and Education: Instructional implications and applications of sociocultural psychology*. Cambridge: Cambridge University Press, pp. 175-205.

Gibbons, Pauline (2002). *Scaffolding Language, Scaffolding Learning. Teaching second language learners in the mainstream classroom*. Portsmouth, NH: Heinemann.

Haasler, Andrea M. (2011). *Peer Scaffolding in CLIL Classrooms – Possibilities and limitations*. Hannover: Leibniz Universität Thesis Paper.

Hallet, Wolfgang, Königs, Frank G. (eds) (2013). *Handbuch Bilingualer Unterricht. Content and Language Integrated Learning*. Seelze: Klett & Kallmeyer.

Li, Danli (2009). 'Is there a role for tutor in group work: peer interaction in a Hong Kong EFL classroom'. *HKBU Papers in Applied Language Studies* 13: 12-40.

Lidz, Carol (1991). *Practitioner's Guide to Dynamic Assessment*. New York: Guilford Press.

Little, David et al. (2007). *Preparing Teachers to Use the European Language Portfolio – Arguments, materials and resources*. Council of Europe: Council of Europe Publishing.

Massler, Ute, Burmeister, Petra (eds) (2010). *CLIL und Immersion: Fremdsprachlicher Sachfachunterricht in der Grundschule.* Braunschweig: Westermann.

Massler, Ute, Iannou-Gergiou, Sophie (2010). 'Best practice: how CLIL works', in Ute Massler and Petra Burmeister (eds), pp. 61-76.

Maybin, Janet, Mercer, Neil, Stierer, Barry (1992). 'Scaffolding' learning in the classroom', in Kate Norman (ed.), *Thinking Voices: The work of the national curriculum project.* London: Hodder & Stoughton, pp. 92-110.

Ohta, Amy (2000). 'Rethinking interaction in SLA: developmentally appropriate assistance in the zone of proximal development and the acquisition of grammar', in James P. Lantolf (ed.), *Sociocultural Theory and Second Language Learning.* Oxford: Oxford University Press, pp. 51-79.

Selting, Margret et al. (2009). 'Gesprächsanalytisches Transkriptionssystem 2 (GAT 2)', *Gesprächsforschung - Online-Zeitschrift zur verbalen Interaktion* 10: 353-402.

Shrum, Judith L., Glisan, Eileen W. (2005). *Teacher's Handbook. Contextualized language instruction.* Boston: Thomson & Heinle.

Thürmann, Eike (2013). 'Scaffolding', in Wolfgang Hallet and Frank G. Königs (eds), pp. 236-34.

Van Lier, Leo (1996). *Interaction in the Language Curriculum: Awareness, autonomy and authenticity.* London and New York: Longman.

Vygotsky, Lev S. (1978). *Mind in Society: The development of higher psychological processes.* Cambridge MA: Harvard University Press.

Vygotsky, Lev S. (2005). 'The genesis of higher mental functions', in Ken Richardson and Sue Sheldon (eds), *Cognitive Development to Adolescence.* Hove: Psychology Press, pp. 61-81.

Wood, David, Bruner, Jerome S., Ross, Gail (1976). 'The role of tutoring in problem solving', *Journal of Child Psychology and Psychiatry* 17: 89-100.

Empowering the prospective CLIL teacher through the analysis of classroom interaction

Maxi Kupetz, Potsdam University, Germany and Rita Kupetz, Leibniz Universität Hannover, Germany

1. Introduction

"Constructionist approaches to education are important because they can help educators understand and change the highly enabling and constraining outcomes that educational processes have" (Wortham, Jackson, 2008: 107). One path in educational constructionism deals with the interactional construction of learning, where institutional learning is constructed in both student – teacher, and student – student interaction, and where content learning is inseparably intertwined with the collaborative accomplishment of classroom activities (Wortham, Jackson, 2008: 110f). The role of language production was stressed in the framework of the Output Hypothesis (Swain, 1993; 2005), which claims that second language learning is fostered when students are actively engaged in the process of language usage. Swain points out the role of collaborative classroom tasks as providing opportunities for the students to "notice gaps in their linguistic knowledge as they try to express their intended meaning leading them to search for solutions" (2001: 60). Long's Interaction Hypothesis (1981) does not only account for the role of input and the modifications made to achieve comprehension and acquisition but also focuses on the negotiation of meaning through interaction, which is essential for any language development (Shrum, Glisan, 2005: 19).

Against this background we believe in the concept that every teacher in general and the prospective CLIL teacher in particular can be empowered through the analysis of classroom interaction in order to understand it better and to cope with the specific challenges faced in the CLIL classroom (Escobar Urmeneta, 2013). Our paper consists of two major parts and aims first to provide an account of features of CLIL interaction and second to show how an awareness of these features may influence trainee teachers' knowledge and attitudes and prepare them for their future work at a theoretical and reflective level. In the first chapter, we briefly describe a few principles underlying *Conversation Analysis* (CA) in order to provide the methodological basis for the sample analyses provided in chapter two. Moreover, we will introduce *action research* as a paradigm for the investigation which was carried out as described in chapter three. Chapter four draws conclusions about (the analysis of) interaction in CLIL scenarios and their relevance in teacher education. Our study is thus in line with the German tradition of applied research on discourse (e.g. Becker-Mrotzek, Meier, 2002; Fiehler, 2002), aiming at using linguistic research results to ameliorate oral communicative practice, and it complies with Königs' request for specific CLIL research and its implementation in teacher education (2013: 50f).

1.1   Principles of Conversation Analysis

Conversation analysts seek to reveal how social interaction is organized, how participants achieve communicative activities as interaction sequentially unfolds (for a comprehensive overview on CA see Sidnell, Stivers, 2013). According to Schegloff, the sequence organization in talk-in-interaction is "the organization of courses of action enacted through turns-at-talk – coherent, orderly, meaningful successions or 'sequences' of actions or 'moves.' Sequences are the vehicle for getting some activity accomplished" (2007: 2). Adjacency pairs are the basic units of those sequences in conversation. Prototypically, adjacency pairs consist of two turns which are accomplished by different speakers and adjacently placed. These turns are ordered within an adjacency pair, which means that an initiative first pair part (FPP) is followed by a responsive second pair part (SPP) (Schegloff, 2007: 13ff). Besides *turn-taking* and *sequence organization*, *repair* constitutes an integral part of interactional organization, as "the organization of repair is the self-righting mechanism for the organization of language use in social interaction" (Schegloff et al., 1977: 381). Participants themselves make problems in hearing, speaking, and understanding relevant and treat these through self- or other-initiated self- or other-repair (for the preference system of types of repair see Schegloff et al., 1977). The notion of repair is highly relevant in the L2 classroom as "there is a reflexive relationship between the pedagogical focus and the organization of repair" (Seedhouse, 2004: 142).

In summary, social interaction is not arbitrary, as communicative actions are structured in a meaningful way by the participants themselves (Sacks, 1992: 22ff.) and they need to be analyzed as such by the researcher using the "next-turn proof procedure" (Hutchby, Wooffitt, 1998: 15) in order to reveal what participants themselves make relevant and orient to in the course of the ongoing social activity. Participants' actions are *reflexive* as they themselves generate the context in which they are interpretable for the participants as meaningful actions (Bergmann, 2001: 921; Seedhouse, 2004: 11). Participants' utterances then are *indexical* in the way that they reveal what context participants orient to (Bergmann, 2001: 921; Seedhouse, 2004: 7). In classroom interaction this means that "teachers prototypically do being teachers by asserting in and through their talk the right to select the next speaker, to nominate topics, to ask questions, to evaluate learners. Conversely, students do being students by orienting to the institutionally specified obligation of answering teacher's questions in a satisfactory manner" (Markee, 2005: 356).

Originally, CA findings were based on everyday conversation; however, there is growing interest in CA in the Classroom (Gardner, 2013), and in CA-for-SLA (Markee, 2005). With regard to CA's applicability to institutional interaction, Markee states: "although institutional talk uses the same basic mechanisms that are available to participants to do ordinary conversation, the distribution of these practices and the purposes for which they are deployed in institutional talk differ markedly from those found in ordinary conversation" (2005: 356). Thus, in classroom interaction, the interactional organization varies according to the institutional goals as there is a reflexive relationship between the pedagogical focus introduced by the teacher and the organization of the interaction (Seedhouse, 2004: 106; 2005: 168). In form-and-accuracy contexts the speech-exchange system is organized more tightly and rigidly than in meaning-and-fluency contexts, whereas the organization of turn-taking in procedural contexts is fairly simple as all participants orient to the teacher having the floor (Seedhouse, 2004: 101ff). The different types of repair used by teachers and students also show their orientation to these varying contexts (Seedhouse, 2004: 141ff). Seedhouse underlines that "one of the most difficult feats in L2 teaching is to maintain a simultaneous dual focus on both form and meaning" (2004: 63). In CLIL interaction, where the main goal is to intertwine language and content teaching and learning, the question arises of how participants deal with this obvious challenge. With regard to small group interaction, Markee points out the relevance of the analysis of fine-grained transcripts for teachers and teacher trainers: "they document what successful language learning activity in small group interaction looks like" (2005: 369).

1.2 Action research in teacher education

Our second dimension of research is related to the implementation and evaluation of a course on *Interaction in Foreign Language Teaching* with a special focus on CLIL. We follow Nunan, who takes a broad view on doing research in the context of course evaluation by claiming that "any investigation which contains questions, data, and interpretations of the data qualifies as research" (1992:

193). Our research qualifies as *action research* (Burns, 2005: 241) in terms of three features: firstly, the participative role of the teacher as researcher and his/her self-reflective inquiry are considered; secondly, the theoretical understanding of a classroom phenomenon – here the role of interaction analysis in teacher education – is aimed at; and thirdly, an impact on the curriculum in terms of possible change is intended. Rita Kupetz is simultaneously the teacher and researcher. The course was developed to investigate the role of interaction and interaction analysis in teacher education, possibly to make a change in the course plan of the M.Ed. Rita Kupetz has been involved in teacher education at university for more than 30 years and identified one of the problems novice teachers have: they know about the importance of interaction for language learning, yet they lack knowledge on how to promote interaction in the classroom. The research question thus is: How can classroom interaction analysis in teacher education make a difference in trainee teachers' awareness of the organization of social interaction and its relevance for (language) learning?

The course *Interaction in Foreign Language Teaching* was taught by Rita Kupetz in an English-language teacher-training Master's course at the English Department at Leibniz Universität Hannover in the Winter Semester 2010/11. The course title indicates that CLIL is tackled from a linguistic and a foreign language teaching perspective, considered typical of German CLIL research (Breidbach, Viebrock, 2012: 6). Moreover, the Hanover approach employs the teacher students' potential as experts-to-be of two subjects. Frequently the collaboration with colleagues from the content teaching methodology department at Leibniz Universität promotes multi-perspective student classroom research in CLIL contexts (e.g. Letz, 2012). In the course under investigation, thirteen German students of English and Education with various second subjects, such as History, Religious Education or Biology participated; some of them had already done their practice phase teaching English at a secondary school in Germany. Part of the course was to watch and analyze authentic classroom data in terms of the organization of classroom interaction and its didactic implications (Kupetz, R., 2007). The following sample analyses shall demonstrate possible findings.

2. Sample analyses of student activities in varying CLIL scenarios

2.1 Purpose, data and transcription conventions

In his 2008 study, Seedhouse shows that inexperienced English language teachers tend to experience problems when introducing tasks in the language classroom, as they lack explicitness in establishing a clear pedagogical focus, either on meaning-and-fluency, or on form-and-accuracy. Seedhouse thus argues that "these complexities and subtleties which cause the problems for the newcomer [...] may sometimes be revealed by fine-grained conversation analysis (CA) of transcripts which may then be combined with video to create a powerful induction tool" (2008: 42). This is also the approach we take: we aim at showing how detailed analyses of video- taped and transcribed extracts from ordinary lessons can provide insight into the complexities and subtleties of CLIL interaction, and thus sensitize prospective CLIL teachers for the challenges that may occur.

Hallet (2005: 12) distinguishes between five approaches to bilingual teaching in Germany:

- branches, where students study one or two subjects through an additional language up to school-leaving level;
- modules, defined as units taught in an additional language, covering various school subjects for a certain period of time;
- epochs, where a school offers certain subjects in additional languages over a specific period of time;
- projects, where content of a subject is dealt with in the additional language;
- content teaching in L1 with materials in an additional language.

The recordings dealt with fall into the category of branches (ex. (1), (2)) and projects (ex. (3)). They were recorded in high schools in Hanover, Germany, from 2003 to 2007 during a number of videography projects at the English Department of the Leibniz Universität Hannover. CLIL had been introduced in these high schools by teachers on a voluntary basis in order to promote both language education beyond conventional English lessons and content learning. During the lessons, English was used as a working language.

The extracts chosen for analysis have been selected to illustrate how typical communicative activities, such as *observing and describing* in an experiment in Biology in English (ex. (1)), *explaining* procedures in Geography in English (ex. (2)), and *changing a form of representation* (from a text to a table) in History in English (ex. (3)) are achieved by students in CLIL interaction.

In order to make the video data as accessible as possible to the reader and to provide for sequential analyses, transcripts based on the *Gesprächsanalytisches Transkriptionssystem* 2 (GAT 2) notation conventions (Selting et al., 2009; Couper-Kuhlen, Barth-Weingarten, 2011) are provided below. GAT 2 is a form-based transcription system where notations are made with regard to the forms that occur, not with regard to their function, e.g. questions are not transcribed with a question mark, but the actual prosodic realization of a unit will be transcribed as shown in table 1:

Table 1:   Notation system (Couper-Kuhlen, Barth-Weingarten, 2011)

transcription symbol	parameter
?	high rising intonation at the end of the unit
,	mid-rising intonation
-	level intonation
;	mid-falling intonation
.	low-falling intonation

According to the GAT 2 notation conventions, each intonation unit is notated in a separate line with a segment number; an intonation unit is realized in one cohesively perceived intonation contour and shows at least one focus accent (annotated in upper case). The GAT transcription conventions allow for a precise notation of prosodic features and voice quality. Aspects of turn-taking such as overlap ([ ) or latching (=) are shown, too. In the extracts shown below, non-verbal behaviour and its coordination (|) with verbal resources are transcribed in a separate line and by using a different font. German utterances are made accessible to the reader by an English translation provided in italics on a separate line. In order to depict the interaction in its holistic gestalt, stills are integrated into the transcript. The student's names and faces are anonymised.

2.2   Biology in English: Observing and describing

The growing importance of Biology taught in a CLIL context at school has been pointed out, as, for example, the 'scientific method' used to do and describe experiments provides space for learning by changing forms of representation (Bohn, 2013: 289). The following extract is taken from a CLIL Biology lesson in English in the 8th grade at a German high school which offers CLIL branches. The students are 13 - 14 years old and have been learning English for four years in a regular foreign language classroom. The teacher is qualified as a teacher of

Biology and English and uses English as a working language in her Biology classroom. In Germany, this double qualification is a preferred prerequisite for CLIL teaching. The recorded lesson's topic is the *human senses* as part of a unit on *thermoception*, where an experiment about feeling temperature is central. The teacher has put three bowls filled with water of a different temperature on her desk. The students are asked to put their hands in the bowls to compare the temperature.

Extract (1) *Human senses: Lukewarm*

```
Participants: Teacher (Tea), Nina (Nin), other students (X)

((Nina is standing in front of the class at the teacher's
desk. Murmur in the background.))

008  Tea: can you put ONE hand in here and the
          OTHer hand in there?
009       1.1
010       ((laughter))
011       0.5
012  Nin: <<p> Okay;
013       <<creaky> uh (-) my > (.) LEFT hand is
          vEry <<all> in a very > cold wAter,
```

Figure 1:   *Nina puts both hands in two bowls with different temperatures*

```
014  Nin: and my (--) RIGHT hand (in)
          (--)|1Auwarmem wasser? >
              lukewarm   water
           |((gazes at the teacher))
015  Tea: LUKEwarm wAter,
016       <<p> (X) TAKE a seat. > ((directed to X))
017       (0.8) ((redirects herself to Nina))
018       YEAH,
019       (0.6)
020       alrIght,
```

Nina puts her left hand in the left bowl and her right hand in the right bowl, and she starts to describe what she feels (segment 13). The change in voice quality to creaky, the hesitation signal *uh*, and the self-initiated self-repair of the prepositional phrase display uncertainty of how to describe the situation. This interpretation is enforced in the next segment (14) where again intra-turn pauses occur, and also code-switching from English to German is used, here to initiate other-repair. Through the rising intonation and the gaze directed at the teacher, Nina signals this German noun phrase as reparandum, as in need of being repaired. Interestingly enough, at the moment of the self-initiated other-repair, the teacher is not even looking at Nina, but the prosody used makes Nina's request for help interpretable. The teacher provides the prompt: LUKEwarm wAter, (segment 15), stressing the syllable *luke* and making this relevant as the reparatum, the repaired item. After a short insert directed at another student (segment 16), the teacher acknowledges Nina's description (segments 18, 20) and asks her to proceed.

```
021   Tea:  can you pUt it in the MIDDle bowl?
022         (2.1)((Nin puts both hands in the middle bowl))
023   Nin:  <<p, creak> Okay;
024         u::h > (0.8) for the (-) LEFT (--) hand
              uhm (it's) oo:ps
025   X:    ((laugh))
026         oo:ps-
027         oo:ps-
      Nin:  it's cOld,
028         but not uhm so cold than uhm than the
              |!THI:S! [water,
              |((twice coordinated head and arm movement towards
                the bowl on her left hand side))
029   Tea:             [yeah;
030         yeah;=
```

Figure 2:   Nina coordinates head and arm movement on her left hand side

Nina puts both hands in the middle bowl and starts to describe what she feels (segments 23, 24). The piano and creaky voice in segments 23/beginning 24, the pauses, and the hesitation signals *uh* and *uhm* signal her uncertainty about how to achieve the description linguistically. While talking, she seems to be spilling water and comments on this using the interjection *oops*. This is taken up by her fellow students, who laugh and repeat the item (segments 25 to 27). Nina then repeats the first part of the adverbial complement and finishes her utterance syntactically, lexico-semantically, and prosodically: `it's cOld,`. In the following segment, Nina makes a contrast relevant by using the conjunction *but*, and then making the comparison to the water in the left bowl. She achieves this comparison not by naming the water in the left bowl, but by pointing with her elbow to the bowl in coordination with the focus accent on the determiner *this*. That the combination of verbal, vocal, and kinetic resources makes Nina's utterance interpretable for recipients is shown by the following overlap with the teacher's acknowledgement token *yeah* (segment 29). Coming back to the comparison in segment 28, it is striking that Nina uses the item *so* instead of the adverb *as* as part of the construction *as ...as*, which is not repaired by the teacher. Obviously in this phase, the teacher orients to a focus-on-meaning context. This also becomes evident in the following extract, where Nina again uses codeswitching as a resource, which is not objected to by the teacher:

```
031   Nin: =and for my (0.7)
032        <<p> |MUSS noch mal
                 again i have to
              | ( (putting her right hand in the right bowl again) )
           <<laughing> (GUCken),>>
                 check
033        ( (puts her hand back into the middle bowl) )
034        for my LEFT hand it's cOlder than
           the | (0.6)
              | ( (points with her right elbow to the right bowl) )
035   Tea: |Other ha:nd.
              | ( (bending her head slightly to the left) )
036        SUper.
037        RIGHT.
038        FINE.
```

Whereas Nina compared how each hand felt in two different bowls in segments 23 to 28, she now compares how her hands, which were in two different bowls before, feel in the middle bowl. Thus, Nina shows that feeling temperature is always relative to what has been felt before. Interestingly enough, she starts in English `=and for my` (segment 31), but switches to German to say *I have to check again* (segment 32), realizing this segment in a piano voice to signal it as an insert. Thus, in this case, Nina uses German in order to account for the procedural aspect, and then switches back to English again, repeating the prepositional phrase from the beginning, but stopping abruptly: for my LEFT hand it's cOlder than the (0.6) (segment 34). During the pause she points with her right elbow to the right bowl. What follows is a collaborative completion by the teacher: Other ha:nd. (segment 35). The prompt by the teacher fits neatly on a syntactic, lexico-semantic and prosodic level. Thus, again, Nina makes her utterance interpretable by using multimodal, that is verbal, vocal and kinetic, resources. The teacher then treats this collaboratively achieved description as appropriate and complete (segments 36 to 38).

This extract reveals how the activities *observing and describing* are collaboratively achieved by the student and the teacher and provides a nice example for the integration of content, conceptual and language learning, as elaborated by Zydatiß (2010). It can be shown that students make use of a variety of semiotic resources in order to make their utterances interpretable and to involve the teacher actively in doing the activity, e.g. by making other-repair and collaborative completions relevant. Students and teachers orient towards the complexity of CLIL interaction by accounting for varying contexts through the deployment of their linguistic resources. In the content-related context, the other-repair is made relevant by the student by code-switching (segment 14) and provided by the teacher (segment 15), whereas in the procedural context related to the experiment itself, code-switching is ignored by the teacher and repair is provided by completing the utterance (segment 35). In this way, the experienced teacher succeeds in maintaining the established focus by choosing a specific form of scaffolding.

2.3   Geography in English: Explaining

Geography is one of the most frequently subjects taught in a CLIL context, frequently used at the beginning of a CLIL branch due to its descriptive nature (Hoffmann, 2013: 339). The following extract is taken from a video recording of a Geography lesson in English in a 10th grade at a German high school. The teacher is trained in English and Geography and uses English as a working language in her Geography classroom. The students recorded are 15 - 16 years old and have been learning English for six years in a regular foreign language classroom. The lesson's topic is *coastal features,* which is part of a unit preparing a field trip to Southern England. The following extract deals with processes of erosion.

Extract (2) *Coastal features: Erosion*

```
Participants: Teacher (Tea), Kevin (Kev), Tommy (Tom)
001  Tea: we then knOw that uhm the maTERial
          is (1.8) treated in dIfferent ways;
002        a:nd is uhm (--) MADE up Into smaller pieces.
003        uh: let us remEmber the different
          ↑PROcesses we we Also had;
004        (---)
005        hOw thEse ROCKS Are (---) pUt (---)
          into pIeces;
006        (3.9) ((looks at the pupils))
007        <<p> (what are) the PROcesses;
008        |KEvin;>
          | ((pointing at Kevin with an open palm))
009  Kev: uh (.) we have corROSion,
010        (--)
011        should i exPLAIN this?
012        (---)
013  Tea: ↑yes;
014        would be NICE;
[...]
018  Kev: uhm corrosion is when (.) sOme types
          of rocks uhm are dissolved by (-) Acids
          in the sEa water;
019  Tea: hm_hm,
020        ((laughter in the background))
```

The teacher asks the students to *remember the different processes* of *how these rocks are broken down/put into pieces* (segments 3-5), which she had introduced during the lesson before. The teacher gives the floor to the first student, Kevin, (segment 8), who names one process: uh (.) we have corROSion, (segment 9). As a medium pause without any uptake by the teacher follows, Kevin self-selects and asks: should i exPLAIN this? (segment 11). It becomes obvious that the task introduced by the teacher is vague, so that the transition between the task-as-workplan (as it is planned by the teacher) and task-in-process (as it is carried out in class) has to be negotiated (Seedhouse, 2008: 93f.). It is not clear what kind of task is introduced by the term *remember*. The student makes his interpretation of *remembering* relevant by suggesting that an explanation is referred to, which is confirmed by the teacher (segments 13, 14). This finding is congruent with Dalton-Puffer's observation that CLIL students are not likely to provide an explanation unless explicitly told to do so (2007: 157). After a short insert sequence by the teacher (segments 16, 17), Kevin provides what he interprets to be an explanation: uhm corrosion is when (.) sOme types of rocks uhm are dissolved by (-) Acids in the sEa water; (segment 18). An *explanation* can be defined as an everyday practice used to establish coherence among various characteristics, outcomes, and causes, a practice being realized in interaction by someone for someone (Stukenbrock, 2009: 161). This is also what can be observed here: Kevin's establishment of the causal relationship between the elements *rocks*, *acids*, and *seawater* is accepted by the teacher through the acknowledgment token: hm_hm, (segment 19).

In the following, the teacher asks Kevin to summon another student to deal with another process of weathering (segments 21-24):

```
021   Tea: and the NEXT;=
022        =now yOu NAME somebody here;
023        so that they WAKE up;
024        and °h and you ASK somebody for the for
           the next prOcess; please.
025   Kev: (TOMmy,)
026   Tom: |uh then there's also corRASion,
           |((directs gaze at the teacher))
027        (--) and corrasion results from large
           waves (-) uhm hurling BEACH material
           against the cliff;
028        (1.5) ((starts gazing at his fellow students))
```

The student Tommy names the process *corrasion*, and provides an explanation quite similarly realized as the one provided by Kevin before, using mid-falling intonation and gazing at the teacher. So he establishes a relationship between the elements *waves*, *beach material*, and *cliff*. In the following 1.5 second pause the teacher does not intervene. Hence, Tommy starts gazing at the class and looking for another student to summon, but then looks downwards in his book, and is encouraged by the teacher to continue (segments 29-32):

```
029   Tom: |so uhm
           |((still looking at fellow students))
030        (1.8) ((looks in his book))
031        [(X X X)
032   Tea: [hm_hm,
033   Tom: |hydraulic |PRESsion,
           |((gaze at   |((puts his left hand at the back of the neck))
              teacher))
```

Figure 3:   *Gazing at the teacher, left hand in alignment with the focus accent*

```
034   Tom: uhm that's when (---) the
            |wAves uhm (1.5)
            | ((small beat gesture with left hand))
            a|trAp and
            | ((both palms face each other, without contact))
```

Figure 4:   *Palm movement as iconic gesture*

```
      Tom: com|prEss AIR,
            | ((brings palms together, palms almost touching))
```

Figure 5:   *Compressing gesture as iconic gesture*

```
035   Tom:  |in crAcks and hOles in the CLIFF;
            |((holding the gesture))
036         (1.5)((brings his hands back in starting position, folded
                  in front of his belly, gaze directed at the class))
037         SO;
038         (2.2)((looks at fellow students))
039         KARla,
```

Kevin names the process hydraulic PRESsion, (segment 33), using mid-rising intonation at the end of the unit, gazing at the teacher, and putting his left hand on the back of his head in alignment with the focus accent. The combination of these resources makes uncertainty interpretable. This also becomes obvious in the following segment (34), as long pauses of 0.75s and 1.5s occur. In alignment with the secondary stress on the verbs *(a)trap* and *compress*, he uses iconic gestures which reinforce the lexico-semantics of the verbs. Again, as shown in extract (1), multimodal resources help the student to make his utterance interpretable for the other participants. The segment ends with mid-rising intonation which projects more to come, and indeed, an increment follows, specifying exactly where the process takes place (segment 35). Throughout this segment, Kevin holds the *compressing gesture*. Mid-falling intonation and the release of the gesture at the end of the TCU make his turn interpretable as being completed. Since the teacher does not intervene, Kevin continues the activity by looking at the class, and naming someone who should continue (segments 36ff).

It is striking that the students in 10th grade are able to fulfil the activities without making scaffolding by the teacher relevant. By using multimodal resources, they make their utterances interpretable without having to use code-switching and they are even able to negotiate task-related, procedural problems.

2.4 History in English: Transforming information from a text into a table

The following sample is given to illustrate how the *change of form of representation*, which is said to be a powerful CLIL scenario (Leisen, 2005), is put into practice. At the time of the recording, the students are in 8th grade and have been learning English for six years. The school does not have a CLIL branch, but aims at developing CLIL modules for various school subjects, such as Geography, Biology or History. The recorded lesson is taken from a CLIL project designed by a teacher of English in collaboration with a History teacher using a CLIL approach with English as a working language. The lesson is taught by the language teacher.

The main task of this lesson is to transfer information from a historical source to a table. The historical source is a letter from a potential Irish migrant to the USA written to his uncle who had already migrated to the USA during the time of the Great Famine. First, the students are asked to read the letter, then to work in groups to answer questions on their worksheets. After that, the groups present their findings in front of the class and collaboratively negotiate what to put in the table which is filled in by two students on a computer and projected onto the wall so that everybody can follow. At the moment when the extract begins, the teacher has just asked the groups to finish and the first group to present its results to show that they have understood the intention of the letter. The teacher has just reorganized the class activity and reestablished focused interaction where all the students pay attention to what is presented by two fellow students in front of the class.

Figure 6: Two students present their findings from a text

Extract (3) *Famine: Crop destroyed*

```
Participants: Teacher (Tea), Natascha (Nat), Patrick (Pat),
student 6 (name unknown) (S6)

014   Tea: Okay (go ahead);
015   S6:  uhm-
016        the QUEStion was-
017        whAt condItions in IREland does the
           letter descrIbe;
018        and it was uhm the ↑mAn wrote uhm that
           their poTAto fields uhm were frEEzen uh frOzen,
019        and all over IREland,=
020        =and potatoes ehm the potatoes they DROPped uh crOped
           were sold by (--) eiqht (-) or nine shIllings,
021        per HUNdred,
022        because uh nobody could EAT (.) they,
023        because uhm they had a FUNgus,
024   Tea: okay STOP;
025        l_l_lets STOP here,
026        let's sort out what we can put put in our TABLE here;
027        you FIRST said (--) the potato crop was all Iced,
028        and we don't know if it if it's ICED in the tExt,
029        because we cOuldn't READ it,
030        NObody could;
031        so maybe it's iced (--) uh but uh what can
           we SAY here;
032        (---)
033        PAT[rick?
034   Pat:    [the crop deSTROyed.
035   Tea: the crop ? PASsive maybe?
036        WAS destroyed?
037   Pat: WAS destroyed;
038   Tea: or uhm yeah;
039        THAT would be a good idea; or?
040   Nat: i think ↓potato crop fAiled ↑is is a GOOD one;
041   Tea: PERfect.
042   Nat: ((turns to the computer and types.))
043        oKAY fine;
[...]
```

The teacher encourages the student to start her presentation (segment 14). Student S6 repeats the question to the class (segments 16, 17) in order to provide her fellow students with background knowledge on what her group has been working on. The utterance in line 18 contains several hesitation markers *uhm* that make a speech production problem interpretable. The first *uhm* introduces the syntactic recycling of the TCU, which means that a new syntactic structure is begun with the noun phrase, *the man*. The syntactic structure is kept until the fourth hesitation marker *uh* which signals the self-repair of the participle **freezen* to *frozen*. Interestingly enough, the student is able to self-initiate and to accomplish self-repair without help from others. The distinction between errors and mistakes made by Corder comes in handy here: "It will be useful [...] to refer to errors of performance as *mistakes*, reserving the term *error* to the systematic errors of the learner from which we are able to reconstruct his knowledge of the language [...]" (1967: 167). The student was able to correct the mistake as she had already learnt the irregular verb form.

The student keeps her turn with an increment (segment 19) and continues her elaboration (segment 20) which again contains self-initiated self-repair of the reparandum DROPped. The turn is kept by a further specifying increment (segment 21), and an explanation is provided (segment 22). Within the students' last unit, the morpho-syntactic error *they* occurs without being repaired, no immediate linguistic correction is made relevant by the teacher. The latter breaks into the student's presentation (segments 24, 25) and explains what to do together next (segment 26). She provides the class with a repetition of what was said (segment 27) and then goes on to explain that the student's formulation *the po-tato crop was all iced* needs correction because the reason for the failed potato crop was not explicit in the original hand-written text as some words were illegible (segments 28-30). So the teacher suggests repair on a content level with regard to what the students cannot extract from the original text. She encourages all the students to find a more general description of what happened to the crop (segment 31), and thus initiates other-repair in order to make all students collaborate in this interactive process. Patrick, a student, makes the first suggestion: the crop destroyed. (segment 34). The teacher immediately initiates repair on a linguistic level (segment 35), which is made explicit by the naming of the appropriate voice. She provides the right morpho-syntactic form (segment 36), which is then repeated by the student which shows that he orients to this utterance as one directed at him (segment 37). This collaboratively established form is positively assessed by the teacher; however, she provides the opportunity for another student to make a suggestion (segments 38-39). The second suggestion by the student Natascha (segment 40) is immediately accepted by the teacher (segment 41).

This short extract illustrates that the pedagogical focus may constantly vary between focus-on-form and focus-on-meaning. The first intervention by the teacher starts out as a repair of meaning; what needs to be repaired is the content that the students transferred from the original text to the table. As the phenomenon that the crop was frozen is not provided as evidence by the source, the students should make an intelligent guess and use a more general expression. However, as soon as an alternative is provided through the verb *destroy*, repair is initiated on a linguistic level with regard to the correct verb form. Other linguistic *errors*, e.g. in segments 20 or 22, are not oriented to.

2.5   Discussion: CLIL approach used in the analyzed CLIL scenarios

In his study on the establishment of pedagogical foci in the English language classroom, Seedhouse found that "[i]t is best to state explicitly what the pedagogical focus is, and it is best to introduce one pedagogical focus at a time, otherwise learners may become confused" (Seedhouse, 2008: 55). However, the analyses of extract (1) to (3) have shown that in CLIL interaction, teachers and students orient to the complexity of contexts as they are able to navigate smoothly between meaning-and-fluency contexts and focus-on-form contexts (Kupetz, M., 2011). In all three extracts, the students make use of multimodal resources in order to fulfill their tasks *describing*, *explaining*, and *transforming information*; they coordinate verbal, vocal, and kinetic resources, and also make reference to materials and objects in order to make their utterances interpretable. Teachers should provide opportunities to practice the use of multimodal resources, and to empower the student to use all the resources available.

The analysis of the examples from different levels of language proficiency (grades 8 and 10) suggests that the quality of focus-on-form contexts changes the longer the students have been learning English. Although this seems to be a trivial observation, prospective CLIL teachers should take this into consideration and allow for the students to make use of resources according to their linguistic capacity, e.g. code-switching, pointing or gesturing in lower level cases, drawing sketches in higher level cases.

3.   Interaction (analysis) in teacher education

The following chapter three provides insights into how prospective CLIL teachers' awareness of the complexity of CLIL interaction was raised in the M.Ed. course *Interaction in Foreign Language Teaching*. In the course, extracts (1) and (3) were used to introduce a sequential approach to (analyzing) classroom interaction and to raise awareness towards scaffolding in forms of repair and collaborative completion, and to study the complexity of navigating between two contexts, constantly changing focus-on-meaning and focus-on-form. In extract (2), the teacher asks the students what they remember, and strikingly, they themselves orient to this introduction of the task as a demand for an explanation.

This extract was used in the M.Ed. course to shed light on the subtle problems which may occur in procedural contexts when tasks are not precisely formulated by the teacher. As will be shown, action research was carried out in order to grasp the trainee teachers' assumptions on the role of interaction (analysis) in CLIL (teacher education).

3.1   Course design

Gnutzmann and Rabe (2013) discuss the variety of approaches to CLIL teacher education in the three phases of teacher education; the approach used at Leibniz Universität is obviously an integrated one where the trainee teachers' awareness for CLIL specific interaction is raised. Videography using classroom recordings for linguistic and educational studies is essential for the trainee teachers' learning process (Kupetz, R., 2007). The goals of the course *Interaction in Foreign Language Teaching,* taught at university in the first phase of teacher education, were to study the opportunities created for language learning through interaction and to investigate the link between interaction and second language learning by studying language-related episodes in video-recorded CLIL classroom sequences. The trainee teachers watched the recorded lessons and were provided with transcripts. After an introduction to sequence organization, they analyzed sequences themselves with regard to context-specific repair forms and other feedback strategies. Among others, the extracts described in chapter two were discussed in the course. Furthermore, tasks and materials, e.g. textbooks, supporting interaction were analyzed and tried out as mini-practice. Mini-practice is defined as a simulated short teaching practice unit in an imaginary setting at university, where one of the trainee teachers teaches and the other trainee teachers participate as learners. Furthermore, the trainee teachers designed tasks and materials themselves. In sum, analysis, critical evaluation and simulation characterize the reflective approach to CLIL teacher education at university.

3.2   Research questions, research partners, research instruments

The guiding research questions were: i) What are trainee teachers' assumptions about the role of interaction (analysis) before and after the course? and ii) What impact does interaction analysis have on trainee teachers' awareness of the role of interaction for language learning?

Two surveys on the trainee teachers' assumptions on the role of interaction (analysis) were carried out in weeks 1 and 14, complemented by a feedback group discussion in week 15. Attitudinal questionnaires (Dörnyei, 2003: 8) were used to find out what trainee teachers think of the relevance of interaction in language learning, the benefits of interaction analysis for teacher development and the scenarios used in the course to support trainee teachers' understanding of the role of interaction. Closed items asking for four degrees of agreement or disagreement were combined with open questions. Term papers written at the end of the course and field notes from the teacher as researcher completed the data.

The course *Interaction in Foreign Language Teaching* had 13 M.Ed. students; ten of them answered both questionnaires, three only the first and three only the second questionnaire. The number of course participants is too small to provide for statistically relevant results, thus figures *7* to *10* show tendencies, which invite further investigation. The code for the quotations from the questionnaires is given in table 2.

Table 2:   *Code for the data from the questionnaires*

code	reference
I, II	questionnaire I (week 1), II (week 14)
(1a), (1b), (1c)	items / questions
A-K	participants

3.3   Discussion of the main findings

A needs analysis was carried out in week 1 in order to identify the participants' prior knowledge. Half of the teacher trainees said that they were familiar with the Interaction Hypothesis, e.g.:

> I have heard about it [the interaction hypothesis], but I am not sure if I remember it correctly. When learning a foreign language not only input is important, the students also have to produce output and interact in the foreign language. (I1b) E

> I knew it...if I'd look at it again I would remember (I1b) H

The comments, however, show that there is a lack of detailed knowledge, which thus needs to be revised for half of the students. Less than half of the participants are familiar with Discourse Analysis/CA. All of the students acknowledge that they cannot or can only partly apply this knowledge to their teaching practice.

The survey asked about classroom interaction analysis as a prospective teachers' method for investigating teaching practice in general (I 8) and for investigating their own practice in particular (II 5), see figure 7.

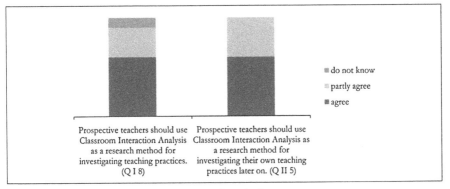

Figure 7:   Interaction Analysis as a research method

Before the course the great majority agreed that it could function as a research method. After the course all of them agreed or partly agreed that it should be used as a research method for investigating their own teaching practice later on. It can only be speculated that there is a kind of long-term effect related to the participants' prospective teaching practice.

Various assumptions on the role of interaction and interaction analysis for teachers' reflections on materials and for their own prospective task design were elicited (Questionnaire II 2-4).

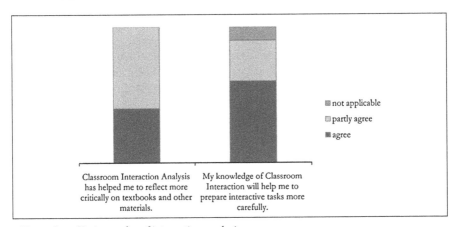

Figure 8:   Various roles of interaction analysis

All students agree or partly agree that interaction analysis helped them to reflect more critically on textbooks and materials. The textbook analysis, on the other hand, helped them to understand better the role of task design in organizing interaction in the foreign language classroom.

Furthermore, a majority thought that knowledge about interaction will help them to prepare interactive tasks. This indicates an awareness of the importance of analytical competence.

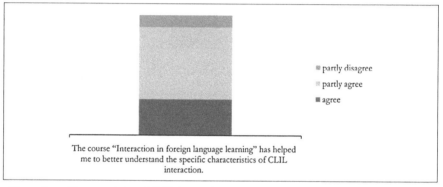

Figure 9:   Characteristics of CLIL interaction

There are different opinions on the implications for understanding the characteristics of CLIL interaction. A large majority agrees that an interactional approach is helpful here, whereas only a minority disagrees. This might be an indication for the fact that there is more to CLIL than just interaction, but an interactive approach is seen as an essential way for trainee teachers to acquire a CLIL concept.

Questionnaire I dealt with assumptions on classroom interaction and language learning, where feedback plays an essential role. All agree or partly agree that the teacher's feedback is important for learner language development. In Questionnaire II half of the participants agree that detailed interaction analysis has changed their view on teachers' feedback practices.

> I realized that teachers can do things wrong themselves if correction is not given in an appropriate way. I also did not know before how important the specific focus of a sequence is. (II 1b) G

> The sessions on repair etc. helped me understand how to give suitable feedback in different in-class situations. (II 1b) L

The other half of the participants do not see change directly, but rather modifications in terms of methods and support in terms of their previous assumptions.

It didn't really change my view on teachers' feedback in general, but it was good to get to know more methods and ways of giving feedback. (II 1b) E

It didn't change, but it supported my view. (II 1b) M

In order to evaluate the course design, the participants were asked whether they agree that the various scenarios helped them to understand better how classroom interaction works. The scenarios used are compared in figure *10*, which presents their perceptions:

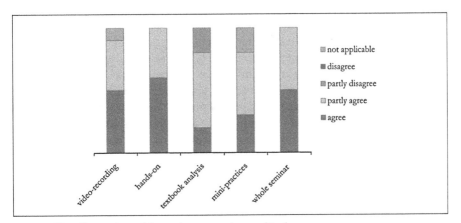

Figure 10: Comparison of the various scenarios used in the course

A comparison of the scenarios and their acceptance and the feedback group discussion with participants shows that

- the hands-on activities offered by the guest speaker were highly accepted;
- followed by the video-recordings and their analysis and discussion;
- textbook analysis is least appreciated;
- mini-practice is perceived as the most controversial.

The various scenarios worked together and the whole course was perceived to be supportive for developing the trainee teachers' interactive perspective.

As mentioned beforehand, *action research* always implies efforts to ameliorate existing curricula, in our case the curriculum of the M.Ed. at the English Department at Leibniz Universität Hannover. Questionnaire II asks whether this kind of course is useful; 80% agree, 20% partly agree. A slight majority agrees that it should become an obligatory component; the remainder partly disagrees. It can be concluded that the course as such is perceived as a helpful component of teacher education; however, the temporal arrangement needs to be reconsidered, as one student states:

> Course is very helpful for students before they do their Fachpraktikum [subject teaching practice phase], maybe include that in the Vorlesungsverzeichnis [lecture programme]. (I did it the other way round, but I got insights that would have helped me a lot in advance of the FP [subject teaching practice phase] → e.g. corrections, explanations,...) (II 8) G

3.4   Summary

In answer to our research question, we can conclude that the course participants were aware of the role of interaction for language learning from the beginning, which is appropriate as this is part of the BA program. In the Master's course, however, they reflected upon interaction by analyzing it in detail and gained knowledge about how classroom interaction *works*. Trainee teachers were amenable to the idea that an interactive approach to analyzing, planning and reflecting on the CLIL classrooms is helpful and that it supports their learning about what is special about CLIL in contrast to traditional language teaching and learning.

A couple of students wrote a term paper about classroom interaction in this course, e.g. Rohlf wrote an outstanding paper on *CLIL in the History Classroom: An analysis of teacher's feedback* , where he stated

> that teachers need to adjust their feedback to the actual pedagogical focus. This can prove difficult, as in some situations language learning is competing with learning history, with one relying on the other. Teachers have to ponder on how feedback causes awareness, touches the learners' motivation and keeps communication from breaking down, so that students can successfully participate in classroom discourse. (2011: 18)

After the course, M.Ed. students appreciated the role of interaction analysis in general, focusing the teacher's role in activities such as questioning, explaining, scaffolding and giving feedback. Thus their awareness of how classroom interaction *works* was raised further by interaction analysis. It must be pointed out that they wished they had had this course before their subject teaching practice phase as they see the relevance for their teaching practice. They would like to combine the analysis with the next steps dealing with methods on how to organize interaction.

4. Conclusion

The analyses in chapter two shed light on the complexities of CLIL interaction and show the CLIL students' and the teachers' ability to smoothly navigate between focus-on-form and focus-on-meaning contexts (extracts (1) and (3)). Extract (2) illustrates how advanced CLIL students are even able to negotiate problems occurring in a procedural context without using code-switching as a resource. In all the examples it becomes obvious how students make use of a variety of verbal, vocal and kinetic resources – as well as objects and materials – in order to make their utterances interpretable and to carry out the activities demanded. Teachers should thus be aware of the enabling power of multimodal resources that students may use to work through activities collaboratively.

Action research in the M.Ed. course deepened our understanding of the design of a learning environment which supports trainee teachers' understanding of the role of (classroom) interaction and its analysis. Our procedure confirms the assumption that fine-grained sequential analyses of videos, using detailed transcripts, provide a powerful induction tool for teacher education in general (Seedhouse, 2008), and for CLIL teacher education in particular (Escobar Urmeneta, 2013). A slight change in the timetabling of the master's course and in the balance of the course components is suggested. It is recommended that this course should be done before the subject teaching practical phase to provide the trainee teachers with a tool for reflection or for their own *action research* during their practical phase. A combination of videography and sequential analysis is accepted by trainee teachers as essential for their understanding; however, these scenarios need to be complemented by hands-on interaction activities, material analysis and mini-practice where interactive tasks and materials are simulated and tried out.

References

Becker-Mrotzek, Michael, Meier, Christoph (2002). 'Arbeitsweisen und Standardverfahren der Angewandten Diskursforschung', in Gisela Brünner et al. (eds), *Angewandte Diskursforschung*. Volume 1. Radolfzell: Verlag für Gesprächsforschung, pp. 18-45.

Bergmann, Jörg (2001). 'Das Konzept der Konversationsanalyse', in Klaus Brinker et al. (eds), *Text- und Gesprächslinguistik. Ein internationales Handbuch zeitgenössischer Forschung*. Volume 2. Gesprächslinguistik. Berlin, New York: de Gruyter, pp. 919-27.

Bohn, Matthias (2013). 'Biologie', in Wolfgang Hallet and Frank G. Königs (eds), pp. 286-295.

Breidbach, Stephan, Viebrock, Britta (2012). 'CLIL in Germany – results from recent research in a contested field of education', *International CLIL Research Journal* 1, 4: 5-16.

Burns, Anne (2005). 'Action research', in Eli Hinkel (ed.), pp. 241-56.

Corder, S. Pit (1967). 'The significance of learner's errors', *International Review of Applied Linguistics in Language Teaching* 5, 1-4: 161-70.

Couper-Kuhlen, Elizabeth, Barth-Weingarten, Dagmar (2011). 'A system for transcribing talk-in-interaction: GAT 2. English translation and adaptation of Selting, Margret et al. (2009): Gesprächsanalytisches Transkriptionssystem 2', *Gesprächsforschung – Online-Zeitschrift zur verbalen Interaktion* 12: 1-51.

Dalton-Puffer, Christiane (2007). *Discourse in Content and Language Integrated Learning (CLIL) Classrooms*. Amsterdam: John Benjamins.

Dalton-Puffer, Christiane (2013). 'Diskursfunktionen und generische Ansätze', in Wolfgang Hallet and Frank G. Königs (eds), pp. 138-145.

Dörnyei, Zoltan (2003). *Questionnaires in Second Language Research. Construction, administration, and processing*. Mahwah, NJ: Lawrence Erlbaum Associates.

Escobar Urmeneta, Cristina (2013). 'Learning to become a CLIL teacher: teaching, reflection and professional development', *International Journal of Bilingual Education and Bilingualism* 16, 3: 334-53.

Fiehler, Reinhard (2002). 'Kann man Kommunikation lehren? Zur Veränderbarkeit von Kommunikationsverhalten durch Kommunikationstraining', in Gisela Brünner et al. (eds), *Angewandte Diskursforschung*. Volume 2. Radolfzell: Verlag für Gesprächsforschung, pp. 18-35.

Gardner, Rod (2013). 'Conversation analysis in the classroom', in Jack Sidnell and Tanya Stivers (eds), *The Handbook of Conversation Analysis*. Chichester: Wiley-Blackwell, pp. 593-611.

Gnutzmann, Claus, Rabe, Frank (2013). 'Bilingualer Unterricht: Lehrerbildung in der 1., 2. und 3. Phase', in Wolfgang Hallet and Frank G. Königs (eds), pp. 102-10.

Hallet, Wolfgang (2005). 'Bilingualer Unterricht: Ideen, Formen und Modelle', *Der Fremdsprachliche Unterricht Englisch* 78: 12.

Hallet, Wolfgang, Königs, Frank G. (eds) (2013). *Handbuch Bilingualer Unterricht. Content and Language Integrated Learning*. Seelze: Klett & Kallmeyer.

Hinkel, Eli (ed.) (2005). *Handbook of Research in Second Language Teaching and Learning*. Mahwah, NJ: Lawrence Erlbaum.

Hoffmann, Reinhard (2013). 'Geografie', in Wolfgang Hallet and Frank G. Königs (eds), pp. 338-345.

Hutchby, Ian, Wooffitt, Robin (1998). *Conversation Analysis: Principles, practices and applications*. Cambridge: Polity Press.

Königs, Frank G. (2013). 'Sprachen, Sprachenpolitik und Bilingualer Unterricht', in Wolfgang Hallet and Frank G. Königs (eds), pp. 46-52.

Kupetz, Maxi (2011). 'Multimodal resources in students' explanations in CLIL interaction', *Novitas-Royal* 5, 1: 121-42. Special Issue: Conversation Analysis in Educational and Applied Linguistics, edited by Paul Seedhouse and Olcay Sert.

Kupetz, Rita (2007). 'Videografische und diskursanalytische Betrachtungen von/zu Content and Language Integrated Learning (CLIL)', *FLuL Fremdsprachen Lehren und Lernen* 36: 76-94.

Leisen, Josef (2005). 'Wechsel der Darstellungsformen. Ein Unterrichtsprinzip für alle Fächer', *Der Fremdsprachliche Unterricht Englisch* 78: 9-11.

Letz, Lisa (2012). *Lehrmaterial für den bilingualen Geschichtsunterricht. Ein Modul für eine 10. Klasse entwickelt, erprobt und evaluiert,* Master thesis. Leibniz Universität Hannover.

Long, Michael H. (1981). 'Input, interaction and second language acquisition', in Harris Winitz (ed.), *Native Language and Foreign Language Acquisition*. Annals of the New York Academy of Science. Volume 379. New York: Academy of Science, pp. 259-78.

Markee, Numa (2005). 'Conversation analysis for second language acquisition', in Eli Hinkel (ed.), pp. 355-74.

Nunan, David (1992). *Research Methods in Language Learning*. Cambridge: Cambridge University Press.

Rohlf, Hans-Christian (2011). *CLIL in the History Classroom: An analysis of teacher's feedback,* Term paper written in the course 'Interaction in the Foreign Language Classroom'. Leibniz Universität Hannover.

Sacks, Harvey (1992). 'Notes on methodology', in J. Maxwell Atkinson and John Heritage (eds), *Structures of Social Action: Studies in conversation analysis*. Reprint (1984). Cambridge: Cambridge University Press, pp. 21-7.

Sacks, Harvey et al. (1974). 'A simplest systematics for the organisation of turn-taking for conversation', *Language* 50: 696-735.

Schegloff, Emanuel A. (2007). *Sequence Organization in Interaction – A primer in conversation analysis*. Volume 1. Cambridge: Cambridge University Press.

Schegloff, Emanuel A. et al. (1977). 'The preference for self-correction in the organization of repair in conversation', *Language* 53, 2: 361-82.

Seedhouse, Paul (2004). *The Interactional Architecture of the Language Classroom: A conversation analysis perspective.* Oxford: Blackwell.

Seedhouse, Paul (2005). 'Conversation analysis and language learning', *Language Teaching* 38: 165-87.

Seedhouse, Paul (2008). 'Learning to talk the talk: conversation analysis as a tool for induction of trainee teachers', in Sue Garton and Keith Richards (eds), *Professional Encounters in TESOL – Discourses of teachers in training.* Basingstoke: Palgrave Macmillan, pp. 42-57.

Selting, Margret et al. (2009). 'Gesprächsanalytisches Transkriptionssystem 2 (GAT 2)', *Gesprächsforschung - Online-Zeitschrift zur verbalen Interaktion* 10: 353-402.

Shrum, Judith L., Glisan, Eileen W. (2005). *Teacher's Handbook. Contextualized language instruction.* Boston: Thomson & Heinle.

Sidnell, Jack, Stivers, Tanya (eds) (2013). *The Handbook of Conversation Analysis.* Chichester: Wiley-Blackwell.

Stukenbrock, Anja (2009). 'Erklären – Zeigen – Demonstrieren', in Janet Spreckels (ed.), *Erklären im Kontext – Neue Perspektiven aus der Gesprächs- und Unterrichtsforschung.* Hohengehren: Schneider, pp. 160-76.

Swain, Merrill (1993). 'The output hypothesis. Just speaking and writing aren't enough', *The Canadian Modern Language Review* 50, 1: 158-64.

Swain, Merrill (2001): 'Integrating language and content teaching through collaborative tasks', *The Canadian Modern Language Review* 58, 1: 44-63.

Swain, Merrill (2005). 'The output hypothesis: theory and research', in Eli Hinkel (ed.), pp. 471-83.

Wortham Stanton, Jackson, Kara (2008). 'Educational constructionisms', in James A. Holstein and Jaber F. Gubrium (eds), *Handbook of Constructionist Research.* New York, London: The Guilford Press, pp. 107-27.

Zydatiß, Wolfgang (2010). 'Scaffolding im Bilingualen Unterricht. Inhaltliches, konzeptuelles und sprachliches Lernen stützen und integrieren', *Der Fremdsprachliche Unterricht. Englisch* 106: 3-6.

Appendix

Summary of the most important GAT 2 transcription conventions from Couper-Kuhlen, Barth-Weingarten, 2011: 37-38

Minimal transcript

Sequential structure

[ ] [ ]	overlap and simultaneous talk

In- and outbreaths

°h / h°	in- / outbreaths of appr. 0.2-0.5 sec. duration
°hh / hh°	in- / outbreaths of appr. 0.5-0.8 sec. duration
°hhh / hhh°	in- / outbreaths of appr. 0.8-1.0 sec. duration

Pauses

(.)	micro pause, estimated, up to 0.2 sec. duration appr.
(-)	short estimated pause of appr. 0.2-0.5 sec. duration
(--)	intermediary estimated pause of appr. 0.5-0.8 sec. duration
(---)	longer estimated pause of appr. 0.8-1.0 sec. duration
(0.5)/(2.0)	measured pause of appr. 0.5 / 2.0 sec. duration (to tenth of a second)

Other segmental conventions

and_uh	cliticizations within units
uh, uhm, etc.	hesitation markers, so-called "filled pauses"

Laughter and crying

haha hehe hihi	syllabic laughter
((laughs)) ((cries))	description of laughter and crying
<<laughing> >	laughter particles accompanying speech with indication of scope
<<:-)> so>	smile voice

Continuers

hm, yes, no, yeah	monosyllabic tokens
hm_hm, ye_es, no_o	bi-syllabic tokens
?hm?hm	with glottal closure, often negating

Other conventions

((coughs))	non-verbal vocal actions and events
<<coughing> >	...with indication of scope
( )	unintelligible passage
(xxx), (xxx xxx)	one or two unintelligible syllables
(may i)	assumed wording
(may i say/let us say)	possible alternatives
((unintelligible,	unintelligible passage with indication of
appr. 3 sec))	duration
((...))	omission in transcript
→	refers to a line of transcript relevant in the argument

Basic transcript

Sequential structure

=	fast, immediate continuation with a new turn or segment (latching)

Other segmental conventions

:	lengthening, by about 0.2-0.5 sec.
::	lengthening, by about 0.5-0.8 sec.
:::	lengthening, by about 0.8-1.0 sec.
ʔ	cut-off by glottal closure

Accentuation

SYLlable	focus accent
!SYL!lable	extra strong accent

Final pitch movements of intonation phrases

?	rising to high
,	rising to mid
–	level
;	falling to mid
.	falling to low

Other conventions

<<surprised> >	interpretive comment with indication of scope

Interactive and collaborative support for CLIL: Towards a formal model based on digital literacy

Ivana Marenzi, L3S Research Center, Leibniz Universität Hannover, Germany

1. Introduction

The ultimate goal of this chapter is to transcend the *how to* model of *Content and Language Integrated Learning (CLIL)* presented in many parts of CLIL literature, transforming it into a more complex model which integrates and makes the connections between CLIL and the wider world of education, meaning making and information technology more explicit. In its presentation of a formal model for CLIL that captures this new state of affairs, the chapter explores interaction in the context of designing CLIL material, focusing on communication, collaboration, and the search-and-share capabilities of new technologies insofar as they facilitate the development of curricula that promote students' conceptual understanding and procedural competences. As many chapters in this volume clarify, CLIL is no longer an activity taking place in an isolated way within the confines of individual classrooms. Rather CLIL is in the process of realising its potential to transcend these confines in keeping with the changed way, in which each and every one of us communicates in today's world. A model of CLIL that formalises these linkages to the *wider* world and its communicative practices is thus in order. Our goal is to theorize on CLIL in the context of *multiliteracy* pedagogy, with a special focus on digital literacy, developing CLIL to meet the challenges of *multimodal representations* in our modern world. The result is an *integrative* model of CLIL.

Section 2 focuses on language teaching and, in particular, on CLIL methodology, describing its links with multiliteracies and the requirements of the new globalized world, suggesting the significance of *digital literacy* in modern society and the reasons why teachers, CLIL teachers in particular, should perhaps take a greater interest in the way digital literacy relates to the subject they teach. Section 3 looks at the role of technology in education and specifically at the way technology support can be expected to affect the theoretical model underlying CLIL. It discusses the support which students, and perhaps teachers and researchers as well, may need, in order to fully benefit from their involvement with technology in an educational environment and the potential for digital literacy to be integrated into the CLIL classroom.

2. CLIL in a world of digital literacy, multiliteracies, multimodality and multilingualism

CLIL is one of the most promising approaches to foreign language teaching and learning to emerge in the last 20 years.

> CLIL refers to any dual-focused educational context in which an additional language, thus not usually the first language of the learners involved, is used as a medium in the teaching and learning of non-language content (Marsh, 2002: 2).

The interplay between cultural and linguistic diversity is one of the key facts of our time that has changed the very nature of language learning. Dealing with linguistic and cultural differences is a central part of our working, social and private lives. Effective citizenship and productive work require us to interact effectively using multiple languages, multiple Englishes, and communication patterns that cross cultural, community, and national boundaries with increasing frequency (New London Group, 1996). In a globalized world, interaction with others requires shared language for communication, so that language learning and teaching increasingly recognize the fact that knowing a language is not just important for personal knowledge, but crucial in modern society for survival (Bossert, 1996).

Internet and new technologies have also changed contemporary society's interaction and meaning-making practices. "New online media are helping to transform language and literacy, with important consequences for language teaching" (Warschauer, 2001: 49). Online communication and other forms of transnational media such as transnational broadcasting, digital TV platforms and channels, are providing non-native speakers of English with greater communicative opportunities. New challenges for traditional school-based teaching, pedagogies and curricula are emerging. Available materials and communicative tools need to be aligned with pedagogical purposes and integrated into meaningful learning situations (Sharples et al., 2013). Even in the mid-1990s, the New London Group authors (1996) already argued for a different kind of pedagogy where language and other modes of meaning (such as images and sound) were considered as 'dynamic representational resources' constantly remade by users as they work to achieve their various cultural ends.

The curriculum now needs to mesh with different subjectivities, and with their attendant languages, discourses, and registers, and use these as a resource for learning. The European Commission is increasingly taking the lead in the socio-political drive to implement new Internet age curricula. Their website[1] recommends the benefits of CLIL in a variety of contexts: "building inter-cultural knowledge and understanding; developing communication skills; improving language competences; developing multilingual interests and attitudes; providing opportunities to study a specific curricular discipline or subject (the *content* in the CLIL acronym) through different perspectives; diversifying class-room methodology, and increasing learner motivation and confidence in both the language and the subject being taught".

But how are these recommendations structured within curricular frameworks or within formal models of CLIL? Working towards a cohesive conceptual tool, Coyle developed the 4Cs Framework in 1999 (including Content, Cognition, Communication and Culture) which differs from the standards-based world lan-guages education strategy focusing mainly on the language curriculum, as it gives much relevance to culture, bringing together language learning theories and intercultural understanding (Coyle, 1999). Zydatiß (2007) took up the 4Cs Framework while defining the curricular framework for CLIL, described in fig-ure 1, according to which the role of language in the CLIL classroom differs from traditional foreign language learning in that language is a medium through which specific subject content is learned and provides a connecting link to the cognitive processes. The language needed for these curricular purposes is sub-ject-related and everyday communicative skills (e.g. service encounters), are of lesser importance (Cummins, 2003; Marenzi et al., 2010).

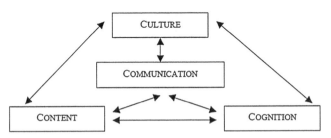

Figure 1:   A curricular framework for CLIL (Zydatiß, 2007)

Cummins (2003) makes a distinction, relevant for CLIL, between two differ-ing kinds of language proficiency that affect immigrants: *Basic Interpersonal*

---

1   http://ec.europa.eu/education/languages/language-teaching/doc236_en.htm

Communication Skills (BICS) are the *surface* skills of listening and speaking, typically acquired quickly by many students particularly those from language backgrounds similar to English who spend a lot of their school time interacting with native speakers while *Cognitive Academic Language Proficiency* (CALP), as the name suggests, is the basis for a learner's ability to cope with the academic demands of various subjects. One of the goals in CLIL is to "help students to verbalize their thoughts appropriate to the subject matter" so as to "boost students' cognitive academic language proficiency (CALP)" (Meyer, 2010).

Supporters of CLIL argue for its superiority over conventional language teaching because of its higher degree of authenticity and frequency of exposure. "Using a foreign language as the working language for the content subject is more authentic than traditional foreign language classroom topics" (Wolff, 2003: 220), and learners become more competent in the foreign language because they are exposed to it for longer periods of time than in conventional language teaching. This raises the question as to whether the time gap between the two types of proficiency described by Cummins can be reduced by CLIL. Further claims relate to the fact that CLIL classroom offers an environment for exploratory learning, as exploring the content subject and experimenting with specific aspects of the subject are natural activities in this type of classroom; *discovery learning* (supported by the work of learning theorists and psychologists such as Jean Piaget, Jerome Bruner, and Seymour Papert) and *project work* are much easier to embed into such a learning environment than in a conventional language classroom (Kupetz, Woltin, this volume). However, critical reflection on these claims, many of which relate to the notion of authenticity, is in order. Research increasingly suggests the need, at the very least, to ground authenticity within a formal model, or system, which includes collaborative searching in social networks and communication with other people in authentic contexts (Kupetz, Woltin, this volume; Blell, Kupetz, 2005; 2011).

It is not only oral interaction which becomes authentic in the CLIL classroom. Interactions with subject-specific materials (maps, graphs, pictures) which are used in the classroom can also be more authentic than foreign language textbooks. Language is presented in real-life contexts in which the natural use of written and spoken forms is assumed to be a learner's motivation towards language learning. In CLIL, however, language is a means, not an end, and when learners are interested in a topic there are strong indications, as indicated elsewhere in this volume, that they will be motivated to acquire language to communicate. The promise of integrating both content and language learning is very challenging, and to be successful, good resources, a clearly defined set of objectives and good task design are essential (Kupetz, Woltin, this volume). Most importantly, CLIL teachers cannot simply *transmit* the contents of a lesson and assume that their students will understand. Rather, CLIL requires an adjustment in methodology to ensure that students understand the subject matter (whether conceptual or procedural), and teachers have to think of other approaches such as group work or tasks, which actively involve students while providing teachers with additional possibilities for feedback regarding the language as well as the subject being taught (Baldry, Coccetta, 2012).

Changes in technology clearly support authenticity in language learning in general. It has often been observed that during the 20th century, the development of language, writing and print, radically changed the way society processed, shared and created information and knowledge (Warschauer, 2001). In the 21st century this is still an ongoing process in relation to digital technologies which are increasingly becoming embedded in popular culture: mobile phones are widely used; TV, films and music are stored and accessed on computers; e-mail and instant messaging allow communication between people across the world; the Internet and websites such as *Wikipedia* or *YouTube* are primary sources of information and entertainment; Web 2.0 technologies, such as social networking, allow people to share resources and collaboratively search or edit online texts. In this scenario, the definition of literacy was bound to change. In 2003 Daley reported that

> [...] to most people, literacy means the ability to read and write, to understand information, and to express ideas both concretely and abstractly. The unstated assumption is that 'to read and write' means to read and write text (Daley, 2003: 33).

Already in 1996, in their manifesto *A Pedagogy of Multiliteracies: Designing social futures* the New London Group authors coined the term *multiliteracies* which addresses *textual multiplicity* as "the multiplicity of communication channels and mass media, as well as cultural and linguistic diversity" (Cope, Kalantzis: 9). Written language, they argued, is becoming more closely intertwined with other modes, and in some respects more like them. Our ability to understand a text – taken as a unit not of form but of meaning (Halliday, Hasan 1976/2001: 2) – has shifted from writing and reading to text construction and communication skills (the focus is more on communicating, interacting and sharing than on reading information as an individual).

As Kress points out (2003: 196), "reading itself is no longer an *interpretative* process, but more and more a *transformative* process, where readers integrate, adjust, divide into sections, and prioritize parts of the text at will". Daley remarks that:

> The very vocabulary of multimedia encourages approaches different from those used to write text. One creates and constructs media rather than writing it, and one navigates and explores media rather than reading it. The process is active, interactive,

and often social, allowing for many angles of view [...] literacy, is no longer only about rules and their correct application. It is about being faced with an unfamiliar kind of text and being able to search for clues about its meaning without immediately feeling alienated and excluded from it. It is also about understanding how this text works in order to participate in its meanings (its own particular 'rules'), and about working out the particular context and purposes of the text (Daley, 2003: 36).

According to Hague and Payton in the Futurelab handbook (2010):

> Digital literacy is an important entitlement for all young people in an increasingly digital culture. [....] To be digitally literate is to have access to a broad range of practices and cultural resources that you are able to apply to digital tools. It is the ability to make and share meaning in different modes and formats; to create, collaborate and communicate effectively and to understand how and when digital technologies can best be used to support these processes (Hague, Payton, 2010: 4).

Embedded in these definitions is the increasingly multimodal or multisemiotic nature of meaning making and hence of literacy. Though in the past literacy has been centered mainly on language, with the introduction and use of new technologies and visual texts, we now encounter, use and interpret multiple kinds of literacies which are embedded in multimodal texts. To learn English at university level, no matter how important grammar might be, the goal to be reached necessarily involves reflection on texts and an understanding of how texts and genres work in terms of making meaning in context (Lorenzo, 2013). How well equipped is CLIL to take on board the effects of contemporary multisemiotic meaning-making processes in which language is not the only and perhaps not the primary meaning-making resource?

Only in recent decades did a distinct field of multimodal studies begin to emerge, demonstrating the need for CLIL to refer to *multimedia/multimodal literacy* in relation to the science of multimodality which studies the relationships between different semiotic resources such as language, colour, lines, shapes and so on, to make meaning (Baldry, Thibault, 2006; O'Halloran et. al., 2010). Analyses of interactive hypermedia, in particular, illustrate the significance of *multimedia/multimodal literacy* (Lemke, 2002). Thus Kellner points out that:

> [...] in addition to the linear cognitive skills needed for traditional reading of print material, multimedia literacy responds to the need to read hypertexts that are often multidimensional, requiring the connecting of images, graphics, texts, and increasingly audio-video material. It also involves making connections between the complex and multilayered cyberworld and its connection with the real world (Kellner, 1998: 107).

Digital media are changing reading and writing practices, giving rise to a new set of literacies incorporating onscreen reading, online navigation and research, hypermedia interpretation and authoring, and many-to-many synchronous and asynchronous communication. "The computer thus becomes more than an optional tool for language tutoring, but rather an essential medium for literacy and language use" (Warschauer, 2001: 49). By way of illustration, figure 2 shows Google+, one of the newest sharing applications by Google. (October 26th, 2013, from http://www.google.com/intl/en/+/learnmore/). The web page is a composition of a Top Bar menu, slogans ("Share and discover, all across Google"), short textual descriptions, buttons and links that open new interactive presentations of the tool (e.g. *Learn more*), frames that show pictures and videos. The reader first learns how to recognize the different objects presented on the page (written text, buttons, frames etc...), subsequently opens and reads the different kinds of texts to collect various items of information and finally, reorders them mentally to grasp the whole picture.

Figure 2:   *Google +: An example of a multidimensional text*

The conclusion may be drawn that a CLIL model that formally integrates competences in multimodality and ICC (*Intercultural Communicative Competence*) is urgently needed. In a global information environment, as *Google*+ illustrates, digital literacy will involve switching from sites relating to one country to others, thus requiring contextual understanding and literacy skills that focus on the ability to read and interact with people through websites from different cultures. The need for CLIL to take multimodality on board in a serious way is an example of an overall goal of modern language teaching: developing ICC (Wiseman, 2003). As shown in section 3, the sharing facilities incorporated within multidimensional texts provide a completely new dimension to the development of ICC within CLIL and modern language teaching in general. To summarize: changes in the contemporary communications environment add a sense of urgency in the deployment of multimodality in learning and in the development of a meta-language which teaches about the design features (i.e. grammars) of other modes in addition to language. Multimedia also requires that attention is paid to design, navigation, and interface construction as does the ICC issue.

In the light of these changes to texts and genres, and the new learning requirements they entail, we need to reflect critically on what education, and in our case CLIL in particular, can offer. The hype surrounding CLIL is perhaps indicative of the need for CLIL to be embedded in the much broader framework of educational, semiotic IT and subject matter theory and methodology. All too often perhaps current research in the field focuses on the structural and lexical aspects of language in keeping with a focus on:

> [...] repackaging information in a manner that facilitates understanding. Charts, diagrams, drawings and hands-on experiments and the drawing out of key concepts and terminology are all common CLIL strategies (Mehisto et al., 2008: 11).

The impression left by many CLIL studies is precisely one in which the focus appears to be on the skilful integration between language and content achieved on the basis of classroom experience that do not satisfy the needs of those who want greater theoretical insights and underpinnings. In other words, there is a problem of understanding how CLIL fits in with (or does not fit in with) mainstream issues in education and language learning.

If learning skills together with content and language are "the three goals of CLIL" (Mehisto et al., 2008: 12), then the failure to explore meaning processes systematically becomes indisputable. An approach which links literacy, multimodality, genre and text analysis to education and meaning making processes is needed to provide a better context for working with CLIL and to implement the European Commission's recommendations. First, the nature of the workplace is radically changing and will require young people to be able to work in teams and to respond creatively to a rapidly changing world. Second, learning is increasingly seen to be most effective when learners work creatively together to build shared understanding (Kalantzis, Cope, 2008).

Generally speaking, in defining the mission of education, we can argue that its fundamental *raison d'être* is to ensure that all students benefit from learning in ways that allow them to participate fully in public, community and economic life (Kupetz, Woltin, this volume). Multiple literacy pedagogy is expected to play a particularly important role in fulfilling this mission. Pedagogy is a teaching and learning relationship that creates the potential for building learning conditions leading to full and equitable social participation. This might involve activities such as simulating work relations of collaboration, commitment, and creative involvement; using the school as a site for mass media access and learning; reclaiming the public space of school citizenship for diverse communities and discourses; and creating communities of learners that are diverse and respectful of the autonomy of lifeworlds (New London Group, 1996: 72-73).

We agree with Cope and Kalantzis when they say that:

> [...] literacy education is about students in our classrooms becoming a part of the global world through mass media, the internet and the multiplicity of communication channels and through interaction with others (Cope, Kalantzis, 2000: 18).

In section 3 we adopt a real life and explorative learning approach where students work collaboratively within a project, collecting and designing CLIL materials. Specifically there is a need to focus on CLIL methodology in relation to the support learners and teachers need during the learning process. In keeping with this chapter's goal, we will suggest the need to deal with the content and collaboration aspects relevant to successful CLIL material design in relation to formal models.

3. What is the role of information technology in language teaching?

> [...] the Internet is an important social environment, rather than a tool or a thing. And it is becoming a major environment in which people use English for reading, writing and interpersonal communication [...] if we want people to learn how to communicate, read, and write in online environments, we're going to have to take them there (Warschauer, 2001: 56).

The success of Web 2.0 platforms (such as *Wikipedia*) shows that people are willing to share resources and knowledge with other people. Popular resource sharing systems such as *YouTube* or *Flickr*, allow users to upload and share content, but do not focus on *educational resources*. Petrides et al. (2008) point out that there is a need for platforms, which allow users to share open educational resources and inspire a culture of continuous improvement of these resources. In addition, sharing of educational material requires an environment which permits the storage of resources in different formats. Almost all Web 2.0 infrastructure, though, focuses on particular media types: videos in *YouTube*, pictures in *Flickr*, or bookmarks in *Delicious*. Thus, despite the variety of available systems, linking distributed educational resources related to the same context is still difficult.

Since the goal in CLIL is to explicitly teach a subject through a foreign or additional language and implicitly to teach the language through this subject, adding collaborative searching is part of constructing the context, and hence making language learning authentic (Marenzi, Nejdl, 2012). The research activity reported in the following sections has addressed these issues by evaluating and redesigning a platform, LearnWeb2.0, to provide better interaction and collaboration support in the CLIL classroom.

3.1   LearnWeb2.0: Interactive and collaborative support for CLIL

LearnWeb2.0[2] is an integrated environment for sharing Web 2.0 resources. It was created within the TENCompetence European project and has been further developed at the L3S Research Center in Hanover. In the following paragraphs we give a short summary of the main LearnWeb2.0 functionalities. More details can be found in (Marenzi et al., 2010; Marenzi, Nejdl, 2012; Marenzi, Zerr, 2012).

LearnWeb2.0 provides several features designed to support collaborative group search and annotation of resources from ten Web 2.0 services including YouTube, SlideShare, and Blogger (Abel, 2009; Marenzi et al., 2009).

Collaborative search. LearnWeb2.0 provides a generic search interface for different kinds of resources (including, in the computing tradition, images, video clips, social network contacts) to match different types of subject-matter. As Kupetz and Woltin (this volume) point out, "Content drives the curriculum", but it is not easy to find good CLIL material for all subjects. "For a long time only social science subjects were favored for the CLIL approach" (Kupetz, Woltin: this volume) because scientific experiments or historical events can be shown in videos and images. On the other hand, it is still difficult to find good CLIL material about Religion, for example, as well as good multilingual resources, because most resources are localized and carry culturally loaded meaning. Using LearnWeb2.0, students as well as teachers can search in social networks and discover authentic resources (i.e. real examples posted by people living in a specific context) that fit a particular learning goal. The LearnWeb2.0 CLIL community can collect and create a valuable repository of CLIL educational resources to be shared with other colleagues and researchers in the field (Mehisto, 2012).

---

2   http://learnweb.l3s.uni-hannover.de/new/lw/index.jsf

Communication and collaboration. Accessibility to a large quantity of information through the Web, though, does not always mean reliability or good quality regarding educational resources. Teachers have the important role of designing good tasks and activities which can help students in developing critical skills and the ability to work online and collaborate in groups. After the resource is added to the LearnWeb2.0 repository, it can be commented on, rated and tagged by all users in the same way as other Web 2.0 platforms. Ratings reflect the relevance of the resource for the CLIL unit. By exchanging comments, the students and/or teacher can discuss resource quality, reliability and usability for the course and collaboratively describe the materials more precisely within the learning context (figure 3). Finally, the selected and rated resources can be used for self-directed learning and re-adapted for designing new course materials.

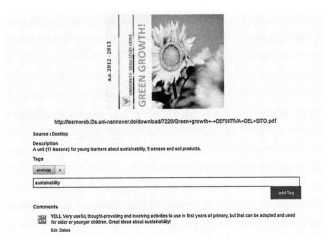

Figure 3:   Annotation and sharing of resources in LearnWeb2.0

3.2   Different levels of design

Teachers and managers are seen as designers of learning processes and environments (New London Group, 1996: 73).

According to the New London Group authors, educational research should become a design science, studying how different curricular, pedagogical and classroom designs motivate and achieve different sorts of learning. The key concept they introduce is that of *Design*, in which we are both inheritors of patterns and conventions of meaning and at the same time active designers of meaning. In our opinion, the role of technology in this respect is to support teachers in designing learning activities in different contexts and to facilitate the monitoring of the learning process.

The *Learning by Design Project Group* (Kalantzis, Cope, 2005) emphasizes the relationships between received modes of meaning (*Available Designs*: how people are positioned by the elements of available modes of meaning), the transformation of these modes of meaning in their hybrid and inter-textual use (*Designing*: how the authors of meanings in some important senses bear the responsibility for being consciously in control of their transformation of meanings), and their subsequent to-be-received status (The *Redesigned*: how the effects of meaning, the sedimentation of meaning, become a part of the social process).

Four components in pedagogy are suggested: *Situated Practice*, which draws on the experience of meaning-making in lifeworlds, the public realm and workplaces; *Overt Instruction*, through which students develop an explicit meta-language of Design; *Critical Framing*, which interprets the social context and purpose of Designs of meaning; and *Transformed Practice*, in which students, as meaning-makers, become Designers of social futures. In this way, we can identify different levels of design and different areas where LearnWeb2.0 can help.

Table 1:   *Different levels of design (New London Group, 1996; Yelland et al., 2008)*

Source	Designing what?	Who?	LearnWeb2.0 contribution
New London Group	*social futures*	everybody	Collaborative search in social networks (*Situated Practice*)
Learning by Design	*course materials*	teachers	Design and monitor collaborative learning activities (*Overt Instruction*)
Learning by Design	*project work*	students	Annotate, discuss and organize multimedia resources and creatively reuse them in other contexts. (*Critical Framing* and *Transformed Practice*)

At school, teachers and students operate within a community of learners and curriculum transformation. Teachers design learning experiences in a cyclical negotiation with students, and students learn from the assigned tasks how to apply design and use creativity to re-design CLIL teaching unit materials. They are encouraged to experiment and to creatively design new meanings in different iterations and interactions with others and with the external world "introducing agency in their learning" (Healy, 2008: 15). According to Mehisto (2012: 16), "Quality learning materials guide students in seeking out and using other resources (sources) for learning". Good search strategies and tools that support teachers and students in finding useful resources for CLIL are needed. The LearnWeb2.0 contribution is to support teachers and students in becoming "active designers of new meanings".

In CLIL all aspects of *digital literacy* (such as collaboration and communication skills, functional skills (i.e. the use of digital technologies), the ability to find and select information, cultural and social awareness and understanding, critical thinking and creativity), are closely interlinked, so that developing one will often involve students making use of others. Hague and Payton notice that:

> When students are successfully collaborating, for example, they are likely to be developing their communication skills simultaneously. When students are thinking critically, they can also be developing social and cultural understanding, thinking about how to communicate with particular audiences, and staying safe. When students are given the opportunity to use digital technologies for these tasks, they will need to think about how technology can be used properly and they will practice and rehearse their functional skills (Hague, Payton, 2010: 46).

As a planning tool, LearnWeb2.0 provides an environment for teachers to go through in order to ensure that a particular task or project includes elements of the different components of *digital literacy*. Table 2 summarizes how LearnWeb2.0 features can support each component. For example, using the Learn-Web2.0 forum to discuss and select resources according to their reliability and relevance supports *critical thinking*, as well as collecting and organizing multimedia resources in collaborative groups and folders helps students in *creatively* designing new CLIL teaching materials for different contexts.

Table 2:   LearnWeb2.0 supporting digital literacy

Digital literacy components	LearnWeb2.0 features supporting digital literacy
Functional skills	Use of digital technologies to support the learning process
Ability to search, find and select information	Collaborative search in different Web2.0 tools (such as YouTube, Flickr, Slideshare)
Cultural and social awareness and understanding	Collaborative search and sharing of resources in social networks (such as Facebook)
Collaboration and communication	Annotation and commenting of the shared resources

| Critical thinking | Discuss in the LearnWeb2.0 forum and organize multimedia resources according to their reliability and relevance for CLIL |
| Creativity | Design and monitor collaborative learning activities through the Logs and activity statistics. Creatively reuse the collected resources in other contexts (e.g. to design new CLIL courses). |

3.3 A learning scenario

> What we need is project-based learning, with students having the opportunity to en-
> gage in learner-centered collaborative projects, working together with their class-
> mates and with others around the world, using a variety of technological means
> (Warschauer, 2001: 57).

A classroom research project carried out during the summer semester 2010 at
the Leibniz Universität Hannover helps illustrate the discussion in the previous
section. The LearnWeb2.0 system was used to support a group of 18 trainee
teachers in a CLIL English seminar (Marenzi et al., 2010). By way of illustration
of our assumptions about project-based learning, the tasks developed – which
were designed to foster students' active and creative learning, in particular those
aspects of learning involving interaction and collaboration – are presented briefly in this section.

> Selecting an appropriate mix of knowledge processes is merely the first step in de-
> signing pedagogy, the next step is to think about students' participation in those pro-
> cesses. There is no point in designing activities to promote selected knowledge pro-
> cesses if students' participation is limited (Dooley, 2008: 115).

In the initial phase of the seminar, students were required to undertake labora-
tory work in order to understand the basic principles of retrieving resources that
are likely to support their understanding of CLIL. Figure 4 shows the activities
carried out in the teacher education scenario in Hanover. To visualize the learning tasks we use a CSCL (*Computer Supported Collaborative Learning*) script
(Dillenbourg, Jermann, 2007).

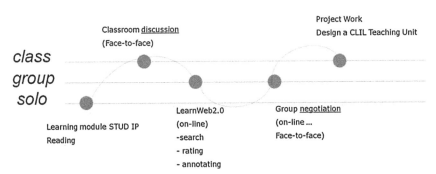

Figure 4:   *CSCL Script of the learning tasks*

Table 3:   *Pedagogical knowledge processes and learning activities*

Scenario in Hanover [teacher education] Methodology Seminar for trainee teachers	
Pedagogical knowledge processes	*Learning activities*
Experiencing the known	Learning module STUD IP: reading and watch video recordings
Conceptualizing by theorizing (CLIL)	Classroom discussion
Experiencing the new, conceptualizing by naming, analyzing functionally	Search and annotation of materials in Learn-Web2.0
Analyzing critically	Group negotiation
Analyzing functionally and critically Analyzing critically, applying appropriately and creatively	Project work. *Assignments:* - Negotiating CLIL materials with others - Designing a CLIL teaching unit/module in small groups

The overall goal of the project work was to further consolidate each trainee's expertise in applying CLIL principles and encourage the process of adjustment and further reflection and discussion. This phase focused in particular on the collection and integration into a lesson and/or syllabus format of appropriate CLIL materials supporting and making explicit each trainee's perception of CLIL and understanding of the constraints and affordances vis-à-vis the shaping and design of materials for CLIL ends (Mehisto, 2012). Following the *Learning by Design* pedagogy, it was the students who determined what resources were worth collecting and including in their final teaching unit, among alternative forms of motivated preparation from the different experiences and sources of material they brought to their learning process.

In Hanover, the prospective CLIL teachers focused on printed media in their material design, however a new appreciation of the meaning-making affordances of modes other than the linguistic was apparent: the focus on the visual was on the organizational dimension of meaning (contents for the teaching unit in the PowerPoint presentation).

3.4   LearnWeb2.0 Design Model

One of the principles of multiliteracies education is that literacy programs must be tailored to particular context: no one literacy program is adequate for all (Dooley, 2008: 125).

In our work we focus on the *Learning by Design* components in the specific CLIL context. Our attention is on the things students *do* in order to produce knowledge. The *Learning by Design* framework operates at three levels as described in Yelland et al. (2008). Table 4 shows the collaborative tasks provided for in LearnWeb2.0 (right column) to support the three levels defined in the *Learning by Design* framework (left column).

Table 4:   *The LearnWeb2.0 approach to the Learning by Design framework*

Learning by Design framework		LearnWeb2.0 approach
Learning elements	Curriculum	Document the sequence of activities made by the teacher and by the learners so that it is a coherent unit based on the knowledge processes exemplified (Material: reading, multimedia resources from the Web)
Learning framework	Pedagogical issues (CSCL scripts)	Learning in the classroom and beyond the classroom using technology (online searching and sharing systems such as LearnWeb2.0)
Learning community	Knowledge processes	Organizational arrangements of documents and of learning. (Discussion, collaboration, negotiation, production (re-creation).

Figure 5 adapts the model described by Yelland by adding a third external circle which includes the activities supported by the LearnWeb2.0 online features (such as Search, Annotation and Negotiation of resources, and creation of a project work). Our goal is to integrate and make explicit the connections between the *Learning by Design* approach, the educational context and information technology (in particular the use of LearnWeb2.0 in CLIL).

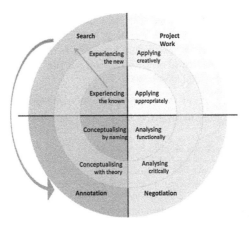

Figure 5:   *Adding Web2.0 features to the Learning by Design framework. (Adapted from Yelland et al., 2008: 200)*

The inner arrow indicates the direction of the support: the *Search* functionality supports the knowledge process of *Experiencing*, both *Experiencing the known* as well as *Experiencing the new*. The *Annotation and (formal) Description* functionality in LearnWeb2.0 supports *Conceptualizing*, the *Negotiation and Discussion* functionality supports the *Analysis* knowledge process, and the *Aggregation* functionality supports students in *Applying* in a new context what they have learnt. As described in section 3.2, *collaborative searching* of multimedia resources in social networks allows both teachers and students to find relevant resources for course material design and to experience authentic language exchange in real situations.

> Effective cross-cultural communication and collaboration, including making effective use of information found in online networks, necessitates a high degree of critical interpretation (Warschauer, 2001: 57).

As the counterclockwise arrow shows, the activity continues with the *Annotation, Negotiation* and *Project Work* functionalities. Using *annotations* such as tags and ratings stimulates students in categorizing resources and conceptualizing contents. The commenting functionality provides a powerful opportunity for peer-to-peer discussions (*negotiation*) and critical analysis of the reliability of the source as well as the relevance of the information retrieved. The possibility of collecting resources in specific folders and re-organizing them for the *project work* allows students to apply what they learned in the course and use their creativity to define new meanings.

> Collaboration is more than just working alongside each other. Collaboration has to do with the joint development of understanding. The emphasis is on transformation (meaning that each participant comes away from the collaboration with new knowledge that has been exchanged by and learned from others) and sharing (meaning that individuals have contributed to, reflected on, and justified opinions and ideas with others) (Facer, Williamson, 2004: 4).

Table 5 shows in more detail the relation between the pedagogical knowledge processes and collaborative tasks provided by the LearnWeb2.0 system.

Table 5:   Knowledge processes vs. collaborative tasks

Pedagogical knowledge processes	*Collaborative tasks*
Experiencing *the known* – students bring their life-worlds into the class *the new* – students immerse themselves in unfamiliar experiences and situations	*Search in LearnWeb2.0* Search for resources in the students' social networks Search for multimedia resources from ten different Web2.0 services at the same time
Conceptualizing *by naming* – students categorize their worlds *by theorizing* – students build mental schemas	*Annotations in LearnWeb2.0* Students use the grouping functionality to collect and categorize the resources: they use tags and ratings to annotate the material and characterize their ideas, also to stress some issues for peer viewers.
Analysing *functionally* – students make logical connections *critically* – students question interests	*Negotiation in LearnWeb2.0* Students use the comments with the group members to discuss the collected resources and select the most relevant material for the project work. They are encouraged to think critically, learn how to reference the source of information, compare and contrast information and distinguish the relevant from the irrelevant (Healy, 2008: 152).
Applying *appropriately* – students put their knowledge to work in predictable context *creatively* – students innovate imaginatively	*Project work* At the end each group organizes the previously selected material to create a new meaning (e.g. design a CLIL Teaching Unit for a different context i.e. their future classroom).

Having described and included new Web 2.0 features into the *Learning by Design* framework, we are now in a position to suggest a new social networking model for CLIL which we call *Integrative CLIL* (figure 6).

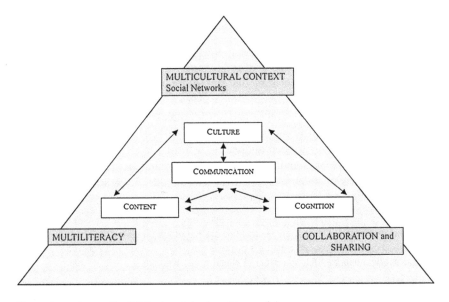

Figure 6:   Integrative CLIL. A social networking model

The *Integrative CLIL* model (Marenzi et al., 2012) expands the Zydatiß curricular framework for CLIL (figure 1), as it considers the global context where the individual interacts within social networks. In this way, communication is increased between different kinds of communities (face-to-face and online through social networks) and personal development (cognition and culture) is enriched by collaboration and sharing with other people.

4. Conclusions

This chapter has presented the first steps in the construction of a formal model of *Integrative CLIL*, i.e. a model of CLIL in which collaboration and sharing are theorized as components which need to be explicitly linked and correlated with digital literacy. The model thus attempts to incorporate issues which are still 'open' i.e. as yet undecided in a definitive way in a global information environment but which, on the other hand, are sufficiently well developed as to require some preliminary formalization. In this view, *digital literacy* is a broad term which includes different digital cultures (as reflected by the growth of information technologies in the 21st century such as digital television, digital cinema, digital music, the Net, video games etc.) and the study of the many new multimodal texts and genres (Baldry, Thibault, 2006; Baldry, 2011) that have arisen. As such, it also includes the need for a diversified *digital literacy* pedagogy within CLIL which provides new activities that stimulate active participation and creative involvement on the part of learners.

Reference to an *integrative* model provides a source of reflection on CLIL and its embracing of *digital literacy*. It can also assist in more practical ways, for instance, as a tool that encourages and guides dialogue with others in the work of CLIL, if only by ensuring that knowledge processes are made explicit by teachers and researchers to their audiences. A formal model can thus help teachers to get across the tasks and activities that they wish their students to carry out with Internet texts in a clear way. In this sense a model helps scaffold the learning process:

> [...] when the knowledge processes are made more explicit, it ensures that teachers and learners are fluent in their use and this has a profound impact not only on learning outcomes, but also on creating a positive classroom climate and becoming confident about being a lifelong learner (Yelland et al., 2008: 203).

A model of this kind can also help out as a guide when developing materials and other forms of documentation for the learning community (e.g. design materials) that can be used by the teachers with their future pupils or shared with the global community of researchers. Although digital tools support collaborative working, a good working environment in the classroom is essential. Before digital technology can be used to support ways of working together, the classroom must be a place for shared learning where all contributions are welcomed and constructively evaluated.

> A culture in which young people don't listen to each other, or discuss fairly the merits of each other's contributions, or one in which their ideas are routinely rejected, will prevent collaboration from occurring at all (Facer, Williamson, 2004: 18).

We have illustrated one way of supporting the model with technology. The LearnWeb2.0 framework (figure 5) helps teachers who want to design activities and appropriate tasks for their students using new technologies. However, it would be wrong to assume that the model and the technology we have presented are the same thing. They are not. Most obviously, the LearnWeb2.0 could be used in non-CLIL contexts such as a community of researchers sharing their work and publications, and equally CLIL contexts could use the model while not adopting LearnWeb2.0 but different tools.

However, there is virtue in developing a tool that is capable of supporting and testing out a theoretical model. In this sense, the current version of Learn-Web2.0 is a redevelopment of previous versions which attempts to incorporate the theoretical model described above. At the same time, it incorporates possibilities of empirical verification of the use made (e.g. through the logs and activity statistics) to reconstruct what went on during the course.

Building research tools into pedagogical tools is in keeping with our starting goal of transforming the *how to* model of CLIL into a more complex model which integrates and formalizes the connections between CLIL and the wider world of education, meaning making and information technology.

References

Abel, Fabian, Marenzi, Ivana, Nejdl, Wolfgang, Zerr, Sergej (2009). 'Sharing distributed resources in LearnWeb2.0', in Ulrike Cress, Vania Dimitrova and Marcus Specht (eds), *4th European Conference on Technology Enhanced Learning (EC-TEL 2009)*. Berlin, Heidelberg: Springer, pp. 154-59.

Baldry, Anthony, Thibault, Paul J. (2006). *Multimodal Transcription and Text Analysis. A multimodal toolkit and coursebook with associated on-line course.* London: Equinox.

Baldry, Anthony, Coccetta, Francesca (2012). 'Group project work in English for Academic Purposes: background research and investigations for a blended course in tourism using Web-as-multimodal-corpus techniques', in Fiona Dalziel, Sara Gesuato and Maria Teresa Musacchio (eds), *A Lifetime of English Studies: Essays in honour of Carol Taylor Torsello*. Padova: Il Polgrafo, pp. 311-20.

Baldry, Anthony (2011). *Multimodal Web Genres: Exploring scientific English.* Como, Pavia: IBIS.

Blell, Gabriele, Kupetz, Rita (2005). 'Vorwort: Zur Situation der Lehrerinnen- und Lehrerausbildung für den bilingualen Unterricht', in Gabriele Blell and Rita Kupetz (eds), *Bilingualer Sachfachunterricht und Lehrerausbildung für den bilingualen Unterricht*. Frankfurt am Main: Peter Lang, pp. 7-14.

Blell, Gabriele, Kupetz, Rita (2011). 'Authentizität und Fremdsprachendidaktik im Dialog', in Wolfgang Funk and Lucia Krämer (eds), *Fiktionen von Wirklichkeit: Authentizität zwischen Materialität und Konstruktion*. Bielefeld: Transcript, pp. 99-115.

Bossert, Phil J. (1996). 'Understanding the technologies of learning environments', *Bulletin* 80, 582: 11-20.

Cope, Bill, Kalantzis, Mary (2000). *Multiliteracies: Literacy learning and the design of social futures*. London: Routledge.

Coyle, Do (1999). 'Supporting students in content and language integrated learning contexts: planning for effective classrooms', in John Masih (ed.), *Learning through a Foreign Language: Models, methods and outcomes*. London, UK: Centre for Information on Language Teaching and Research, pp. 46-62.

Coyle, Do (2006). 'Developing CLIL: towards a theory of practice', *Monograph* 6, 5-29.

Cummins, James (2003). 'BICS and CALP: origins and rationale for the distinction', in Christine Bratt Paulston and Richard G. Tucker (eds), *Sociolinguistics: The essential readings*. London: Blackwell, pp. 322-28.

Daley, Elizabeth (2003). 'Expanding the concept of literacy'. *EDUCAUSE Review* 38, 2: 32-40.

Dillenbourg, Pierre, Jermann, Patrick (2007). 'Designing integrative scripts', in Frank Fischer, Ingo Kollar, Heinz Mandl and Jörg M. Haake (eds), *Scripting Computer-Supported Collaborative Learning*. Boston, MA: Springer, pp. 275-301.

Dooley, Karen (2008). 'Multiliteracies and pedagogies of new learning for students of English as an additional language', in Annah Healy (ed.), *Multiliteracies and Diversity in Education*. Oxford: Oxford University Press, pp. 102-125.

Exley, Beryl (2008). 'Communities of learners: early years students, new learning pedagogy, and transformations', in Annah Healy (ed.), *Multiliteracies and Diversity in Education. New pedagogies for expanding landscapes*. Oxford: Oxford University Press, pp. 126-143.

Facer, Keri, Williamson, Ben (2004). *Designing Technologies to Support Creativity and Collaboration - A handbook from Futurelab*. October 2013, retrieved from http://archive.futurelab.org.uk/ resources/documents/handbooks/creativity_and_collaboration.pdf.

Hague, Cassie, Payton, Sarah (2010). *Digital Literacy across the Curriculum - A futurelab handbook*. August 2013, retrieved from http://www2.futurelab.org.uk/resources/documents/handbooks/digital_lite racy.pdf.

Halliday, Michael A. K., Hasan, Ruqaiya (1976). *Cohesion in English*. Beijing: Foreign Language Teaching and Research Press.

Healy, Annah (2008). 'Expanding student capacities. Learning by design pedagogy', in Annah Healy (ed.), *Multiliteracies and Diversity in Education*. Oxford: Oxford University Press, pp. 2-29.

Kalantzis, Mary, Cope, Bill (2005). 'Introduction: The Learning by design approach', in Mary Kalantzis, Bill Cope and the Learning by Design Project Group (eds), *Learning by Design*. Altona, VIC: Victorian Schools and Common Ground Publishing, pp. v-xi.

Kalantzis, Mary, Cope, Bill (2008). 'Language education and multiliteracies', in Stephen May and Nancy H. Hornberger (eds), *Encyclopedia of Language and Education*. 2nd Edition, Vol. 1, Language Policy and Political Issues in Education. New York, NY: Springer, pp. 195-211.

Kalantzis, Mary, Cope, Bill, Cloonan, Anne (2010). 'A multiliteracies perspective on the new literacies', in Elizabeth A. Baker and Donald J. Leu (eds), *The New Literacies: Multiple perspectives on research and practice*. New York: The Guilford Press, pp. 61-87.

Kellner, Douglas (1998). 'Multiple literacies and critical pedagogy in a multicultural society', *Educational Theory* 48, 1: 103-22.

Kress, Gunther (2003). *Literacy in the New Media Age*. Routledge, London.

Lemke, Jay L. (2002). 'Travels in hypermodality', *Visual Communication* 1, 3: 299-325.

Lemke, Jay L. (2006). 'Towards critical multimedia literacy: technology, research, and politics', in Michael McKenna, David Reinking, Linda D. Labbo and Ronald D. Kieffer (eds), *International Handbook of Literacy & Technology*. Mahwah, NJ: Lawrence Erlbaum, pp. 3-14.

Lorenzo, Francisco (2013). 'Genre-based curricula: multilingual academic literacy in content and language integrated learning', *International Journal of Bilingual Education and Bilingualism* 16, 3: 375-388.

Marenzi, Ivana, Abel, Fabian, Zerr, Sergej, Nejdl, Wolfgang (2009). 'Social sharing in LearnWeb2.0', *International Journal of Continuing Engineering Education and Life-Long Learning (IJCEELL)* 19, 4-5-6: 276-290.

Marenzi, Ivana, Kupetz, Rita, Nejdl, Wolfgang, Zerr, Sergej (2010). 'Supporting active learning in CLIL through collaborative search', in Xiangfeng Luo et al. (eds), *9th International Conference on Web-based Learning (ICWL 2010)*. Heidelberg: Springer, pp. 200-09.

Marenzi, Ivana, Baldry, Anthony, Nejdl, Wolfgang (2012). 'Towards an integrative approach for CLIL: the LearnWeb2.0 model', in Gabriele Blell and Christiane Lütge (eds), *Fremdsprachendidaktik und Lehrerbildung: Konzepte, Impulse, Perspektiven*. Berlin: LIT, pp. 95-112.

Marenzi, Ivana, Nejdl, Wolfgang (2012). 'I search therefore I learn. Supporting active and collaborative learning in language teaching', in Alexandra

Okada, Teresa Connolly and Peter Scott (eds), *Collaborative Learning 2.0: Open Educational Resources.* IGI Global, pp. 103-25.

Marenzi, Ivana, Zerr, Sergej (2012). 'Multiliteracies and active learning in CLIL: the development of LearnWeb2.0', *IEEE Transactions on Learning Technologies (TLT)* 5, 4: 336-48.

Marsh, David (2002). *CLIL/EMILE – The European Dimension. Actions, trends and foresight potential.* Public Services Contract DG EAC: European Commission. Jyväskylä, Finland: UniCOM, Continuing Education Centre, University of Jyväskylä.

Mehisto, Peeter, Marsh, David, Frigols, María Jesús (2008). *Uncovering CLIL. Content and language integrated learning in bilingual and multilingual education.* Oxford: Macmillan.

Mehisto, Peeter (2012). 'Criteria for producing CLIL learning material', *Encuentro* 21: 15-33.

Meyer, Oliver (2010). 'Towards quality-CLIL: successful planning and teaching strategies', *Puls* 33: 11-29.

New London Group (1996). 'A pedagogy of multiliteracies: designing social futures', *Harvard Educational Review* 66, 1: 60-92.

O'Halloran, Kay L., Smith, Bradley A. (in press). 'Multimodal text analysis', in Carol A. Chapelle (ed.), *Encyclopedia of Applied Linguistics.* New Jersey: Wiley-Blackwell.

O'Halloran, Kay L. (in press). 'Multimodal discourse analysis', in Ken Hyland and Brian Paltridge (eds), *Companion to Discourse Analysis.* London: Continuum.

O'Halloran, Kay L., Tan, Sabine, Smith, Bradley A., Podlasov, Alexey (2010). 'Challenges in designing digital interfaces for the study of multimodal phenomena', *Information Design Journal* 18, 1: 2-12.

Petrides, Lisa, Nguyen, Lilly, Kargliani, Anastasia, Jimes, Cynthia (2008). 'Open educational resources: inquiring into author reuse behaviors', in Pierre Dillenbourg and Marcus Specht (eds). *Proceedings of the 3rd European Conference on Technology Enhanced Learning (EC-TEL 2008).* Heidelberg: Springer, pp. 344-53.

Sharples Mike, McAndrew, Patrick, Weller, Martin, Ferguson, Rebecca, Fitz-Gerald, Elizabeth, Hirst, Tony, Gaved, Mark (2013). *Innovating Pedagogy 2013: Open university innovation report 2.* Milton Keynes: The Open University. 31 March 2014, retrieved from http://www.open.ac.uk/personalpages/mike.sharples/Reports/Innovating_ Pedagogy_report_2013.pdf.

Warschauer, Mark (2001). 'Millennialism and media: language, literacy, and technology in the 21st century', *AILA Review* 14, 49-59.

Wiseman, Richard L. (2003). 'Intercultural communication competence', in William B. Gudykunst (ed.), *Cross-Cultural and Intercultural Communication*. Thousand Oaks: Sage, pp. 191-208.

Wolff, Dieter (2003). 'Content and language integrated learning: a framework for the development of learner autonomy', in David Little, Jennifer Ridley and Ema Ushioda (eds), *Learner Autonomy in the Foreign Language Classroom: Teacher, learner, curriculum and assessment*. Dublin: Authentik, pp. 211-222.

Yelland, Nicola, Cope, Bill, Kalantzis, Mary (2008). 'Learning by design: creating pedagogical frameworks for knowledge building in the twenty-first century', *Asia-Pacific Journal of Teacher Education* 36, 3: 197-213.

Zydatiß, Wolfgang (2007). 'Bilingualer Fachunterricht in Deutschland: eine Bilanz', *FLuL Fremdsprachen Lehren und Lernen* 36, 8-25.

CLIL: Approaching content through communicative interaction[1]

Jana Roos, University of Paderborn, Germany

1. Introduction

One main reason why Content and Language Integrated Learning (CLIL) has gained popularity as a teaching approach in Europe is that its implementation is seen as a chance to develop the learning of both content and language (Wolff, 2005). It has been shown that learning subject matter in the target language significantly increases learners' exposure to that language and offers possibilities for its authentic and meaningful use (Lyster, 2007: 2; Nikula et al., 2013: 71). In this sense, communicative interaction plays a central role in CLIL. Not only does it stimulate language learning processes by providing opportunities for negotiation of meaning, but it also makes it possible to take other general principles of CLIL into account, as it allows for an active role for the learner and can help to create contexts for learning by construction (Kupetz, Woltin, this volume).

This paper presents and discusses an approach to content learning through communicative interaction, which combines the key principles of CLIL with a task-based pedagogical design. The first part focuses on language use and communication in CLIL, examining how their roles are reflected in research and in CLIL learning materials. The second part outlines the relationship between CLIL and a task-based approach to teaching and learning. Here, the discussion will focus on the potential of task-based communicative interaction to initiate learning processes of the 4Cs – communication, content, cognition and culture (Coyle et al., 2010). The final part presents data from a small-scale classroom study which illustrates some of the possibilities of integrating communicative tasks (Ellis, 2003; 2009) into the CLIL classroom.

1   I would like to thank Lea Hartung and Johanna Bußwinkel for their assistance with data collection, transcription and analysis.

2. Language use and communicative interaction in CLIL

In CLIL, learners engage with language through content and develop it through its use in authentic contexts. In the 4Cs framework (Coyle et al., 2010), communication is conceptualized as being one of four interrelated building blocks, alongside content, cognition and culture (figure 1). The underlying idea is that the integration of the 4Cs allows for the development of a holistic view and makes learning in the CLIL context "different from regular language or content lessons" (Coyle et al., 2010: 55). The "approach to developing language through use" (Coyle et al., 2010: 59) adopted here runs parallel to the action-oriented view of language learning taken in the Common European Framework of Reference for Languages (CEFR), where the language learner is seen as being "in the process of becoming a language user" (Council of Europe, 2001: 43). Seen from this perspective, CLIL opens up possibilities for meaningful language use and communicative interaction in situations where the focus is on meaning and content. At the same time, situations in which learners are engaged in getting their messages across provide opportunities for such elements as the negotiation of meaning and corrective feedback, which have been shown to drive second language acquisition forward (Lightbown, Spada, 2013; Mackey, 1999; Long, 1996).

- **content** learning implies progression in new knowledge, skills and understanding
- **communication** involves interaction and leads to progression in language use and learning
- **cognition** refers to learners' engagement in thinking processes, allowing them to construct their own understanding
- **culture** in CLIL is related to the idea that understanding the concept of "otherness" leads to a deeper understanding of "self" (Byram 2008) and to progression towards pluricultural understanding.

Figure 1:   Content, communication, cognition and culture in the 4Cs framework (Coyle et al., 2010: 53ff; Coyle, 2005: 5)

Given these advantages, the question that arises, is what role communicative interaction plays in CLIL classrooms (Pica, 2002; Nikula et al., 2013). In the following, this question will be explored both with regard to CLIL classroom research and practice. We shall be looking first at what research reveals about language use in the classroom and then at typical examples of activities designed for the CLIL classroom.

3. Communication in the classroom

An important reference point for CLIL is the Canadian Immersion project, where the concept of teaching content through a second language first took form. This approach has led to positive results with regard to both language and content learning (for an overview see Wesche, 2002). However, as Swain (1993; 2000) concluded from her research in Canadian immersion programmes, content teaching often does not provide many opportunities for student production. This led her to propose the "Output Hypothesis" (1985), which states that "through producing language, [...] language acquisition/learning may occur." (Swain, 1993: 159) The idea behind this hypothesis is that producing comprehensible output provides learners with opportunities to find out about the limits of their knowledge of the target language, to test hypotheses and try out the language available to them. In keeping with this, Lyster (2007: 5) underlines that "instructional practices that emphasize discourse and the use of language as an instrument for learning have much to contribute to improving the second language learning environment in immersion classes."

3.1 Language use in the CLIL-context

The lack of in-class opportunities for language production that Swain observed in the Canadian context seems to have certain parallels in the European CLIL context. As research shows, CLIL classrooms often "tend to be teacher-centred" (Bonnet, 2012: 67) and characterised by whole-class interaction (Nikula et al., 2013). Dalton-Puffer's (2007) research reveals that speaking is generally not promoted in many CLIL classrooms (Meyer, 2010: 13; Coyle et al., 2010).

The reasons for this seem to be manifold and are influenced by both classroom management and discourse. One possible explanation may be the prevalence of traditional teacher-centred approaches in the classroom, which "conceptualise the subject as a body of knowledge to be transferred from teacher to learner" (Coyle, 2002: 27) or "from expert to novice" (Coyle, 2005: 5; Bogaert et al., 2006). Dalton-Puffer, in her research on CLIL in Austria, mentions the limited L2 competence of teachers as another factor. It leads teachers to stick to the intended lesson plan and results in "whole-class discussions narrowly kept on track." (Dalton-Puffer, 2011: 189f.; 2007) As regards classroom discourse and learner output, Dalton-Puffer further states that "students most frequently employ their active language skills in answering teacher questions." (Dalton-Puffer, 2007: 11) Her analysis of the interrelation between teacher-questions and student-responses shows that teachers' questions are to a large extent questions about facts. They typically lead to short, minimalist student answers (Dalton-Puffer, 2006; 2007) and thus to a type of exchange which constrains communication.

3.2   Activities in textbooks for CLIL

Another reason for students' limited opportunities to use the target language in meaningful communication may be related to the types of activities that can be found in textbooks used in the CLIL classroom, and the respective learning goals and assessment criteria with which they are associated. It must be noted that hardly any materials or textbooks for CLIL were available for a long time (Wolff, 2005). With the growing popularity of CLIL, however, more materials have been developed and have found their way into the classroom. In textbooks for different CLIL subjects, it is common for the instructions to be based on can-do statements or learning goals (UCLES, 2011). For instance in geography, learners could be asked to describe and explain the causes and effects of earthquakes, or to compare the climate in two different geographical areas or climate zones (Appleby et al., 2007; Hallet, 2010).

Table 1:   *Activities in textbooks for geography, history and biology, designed for the German CLIL classroom (Appleby et al., 2007; Speidel and Dietz, 2009; Theis et al., 2009)*

TEXTBOOK / ACTIVITY	Geography Diercke Geography Volume 1 (Grade 8)	History Klett Geschichte und Geschehen (Grade 8)	Biology Klett Biologie: Prisma Bilingual (Grade 8-10)
Explain...	how the tropical circulation system works	how the use of steam power changed the cotton industry	why do you think transduction takes place?
Describe...	the effects of the earthquake of 1995 on Kobe	the way the locomobile works	the differences between the visual fields of a wolf and a hare
Compare...	the crust with the mantle and the outer core with the inner core (structure of the earth)	the ward republics to our German system of local, regional, state and federal government	the sense of hearing and the sense of balance
Discuss...	whether it is profitable for a shoe company in Taiwan to move its production to China	the advantages and disadvantages of Ford's assembly line for the workers, entrepreneurs and the consumers	potential sources of danger

While these and similar activities lead learners to demonstrate their existing knowledge of subject-specific content and language (UCLES, 2011: 9; Meyer, 2010), they often do not directly involve learners in communicative interaction in meaningful pair or group work. Even the activity of discussion, which Pica (2002: 39) found to be "the most frequently implemented interactional activity" in content-based classrooms, often does not promote the kinds of interaction that lead to negotiation of meaning and involve learners in the co-construction of content. According to Dalton-Puffer (2011: 191), however, it is especially the process of negotiation of meaning, which "provides an excellent basis for a content-and-language approach, given that school subjects are talked into being during lessons."

Thus, while the concept of CLIL naturally entails a strong focus on language use, its potential for language learning cannot be fully exploited if opportunities for learners to engage in collaborative and communicative activities are rare. Hence, with regard to her findings in the area of classroom discourse in CLIL, Dalton-Puffer (2007: 11) concludes that students' use of the target language is much more limited than expected and creative language use is often "severely limited or non-existent". This leads to the question of how one can create learning scenarios that offer students the possibility to use the language actively in authentic communication. In this context, task-based language teaching seems to be a promising approach.

4. Task-based Learning and CLIL

Task-based language teaching has become increasingly popular because of the possibilities it offers to promote second language acquisition and the development of communicative competence in the foreign language classroom. Tasks provide learners with opportunities to use the linguistic means available to them in order to convey information and to achieve a clearly defined outcome (Ellis, 2003; 2009: 223). Thus, they engage learners in communicative language use in situations in which the focus is on meaning and content. What becomes apparent here is that task-based language teaching shares key principles with CLIL: in both approaches, there is a primary focus on meaning and both explore "the relationship between language learning and the content within which it is situated." (Coyle et al., 2010: 54) The resulting interactional episodes provide opportunities for negotiation of meaning and corrective feedback and can "draw students' attention to form in relation to content meaning." (Pica, 2002: 37) Coyle et al. point to possible benefits of using tasks in the CLIL classroom by saying that "successful CLIL modules have often included a great amount of paired work, group work and cooperative learning techniques such as jigsaw tasks." (Coyle et al., 2010: 88).

What makes the use of tasks in the CLIL classroom especially relevant in the context of this paper is that tasks have the capacity to promote participation in meaning-based, negotiated interaction in which learners co-construct content (Nikula et al., 2013: 76; Doughty, Williams, 1998). While the lack of cooperative learning formats and communicative language use in CLIL, as described in the previous chapter, indicate that a task-based methodology has not been implemented widely in the CLIL classroom, the advantages of tasks seem to be clearly acknowledged in the field of CLIL (also UCLES 2011). Meyer highlights the potential of tasks for CLIL:

> The relationship between CLIL and TBLT is symbiotic: authentic and meaningful content is used to create motivating and challenging tasks. Authentic communication in different cooperative formats […] and the frequent negotiation of meaning necessary to complete them enables a greater depth and bandwidth of content learning (Meyer, 2010: 19).

Tasks, thus, promote the development of language *of*, *for* and *through* learning (Coyle et al., 2010), as "students acquire the language they need when they need it in order to accomplish the task" (Larsen-Freeman, Anderson, 2011: 150). In line with this, it is claimed that the use of tasks in the CLIL context can provide opportunities for learners to approach content through communicative interaction. It should be pointed out, however, that what is being proposed is not merely the superimposition of a conventional approach to language teaching on the CLIL scenario. Rather, it is argued that tasks can match the demands of a CLIL learning environment if they are designed in a manner that will promote communication simultaneously with content, cognition and culture. In the following, I shall be presenting some findings from a study based on the use of "CLIL tasks". The aim is to demonstrate how such tasks can be developed and used in order to create more fulfilling learning scenarios.

5. Using interactive CLIL tasks: A small-scale study

The use of communicative tasks in CLIL learning scenarios was investigated in a small-scale study. The underlying research question in this context was: can tasks create opportunities for learners to approach content through communicative interaction and initiate learning processes of the 4Cs – communication, content, cognition and culture? The study aimed at investigating if tasks designed for this specific purpose achieved these aims. In order to do so, a qualitative analysis of the kind of learner interaction elicited through task performance was carried out.

The study involved twelve German learners of English as a foreign language at secondary level from two different classes at two different schools. The focus was on Geography as a CLIL subject. All learners were 13 to 14 years old, in grade 8, and had been studying English for 6 years and geography as a CLIL subject for 2 years. In both classes, the textbook "Diercke Geography for bilingual classes" (Appleby et al., 2007) was used, suggesting that a common basis could be expected with regard to the learners' content knowledge and content-specific language.

In the following, the background for the development of CLIL tasks will be outlined. Thereafter, an example of a CLIL task designed for the study will be presented and the interaction between learners elicited by the task will be discussed.

5.1   Applying the 4Cs model to CLIL task design

In order to create a learning environment which allows for progression in content and language learning and integrates the cognitive and the cultural dimension, the 4Cs framework served as a tool for the design of the CLIL tasks used in the study. Even though the 4Cs "do not exist as separate elements" (Coyle et al., 2010: 55), but are complementary to each other, they will be looked at individually here in order to illustrate how the learning processes associated with them can be promoted through task design (figure 2).

Communication

With regard to communication, research shows that the extent and the nature of interaction initiated by tasks strongly depend on the type of task that has been chosen. Goal-oriented tasks, in which information needs to be exchanged between learners, lead to a high degree of interaction and negotiation of meaning (Mackey, 1994). In this regard, Swain highlights the importance of positive interdependence between learners: "each participant depends in some way on others in the group to learn and complete the task. Positive interdependence fosters interaction and ensures that all group members profit from the collaborative activity." (Swain, 1993: 162) This is why jigsaw tasks were chosen as a suitable task format in the study presented here. In this type of task, different learners have different pieces of information that they need to put together in order to reach a common goal (Ellis, 2003). This process creates opportunities for meaningful interaction among learners.

Content

As far as content is concerned, tasks should be based on content matter dealt with in the respective CLIL subject. They should provide opportunities for learners to use content language and subject-specific vocabulary for real purposes in a collaborative context, as e.g. when contributing to joint problem-solving.

Cognition

As for cognition, CLIL tasks should engage learners in thinking processes, such as hypothesising and analysing, and encourage them to explain their reasoning in order to challenge them cognitively and to allow them to actively construct their own understanding (Mehisto, 2012: 22; Coyle et al., 2010: 58). The latter idea is emphasized by Marsh et al. who refer to CLIL as "education through *construction*, rather than *instruction*." (Marsh et al., 2005: 6) In his account on criteria for quality CLIL materials, Mehisto states that "CLIL materials avoid asking students to report back on fact-based questions, but instead focus on having students apply, analyse, evaluate and create something based on the information presented in the materials." (Mehisto, 2012: 23)

Both content and language learning goals come together as learners use CLIL language and content-specific vocabulary spontaneously and meaningfully, as well as the language required to engage in pair or group work. At the same time, collaborative problem-solving engages learners cognitively (also Hallet, 2013). In addition, the fourth C, culture, which Coyle et al. (2010: 54) see as a central element in CLIL, should be integrated when designing tasks for the CLIL classroom.

Culture

While the cultural dimension may be inherent in many of the CLIL materials presented to learners, the corresponding activities may not always provide opportunities for them to explore it (table 1). As Coyle et al. state, culture in CLIL is "sometimes referred to as the 'forgotten C'" (Coyle et al., 2010: 54). This is also reflected in Breidbach and Viebrock's review of CLIL research in Germany, in which they conclude with regard to intercultural learning, that "it has not been examined satisfactorily" in empirical research (Breidbach, Viebrock, 2012: 11). As for task design, the aim was therefore to create tasks that promote the development of learners' intercultural competence and their ability to empathise by making it possible for them to personalise the content and make connections between their own world and the global community (Mehisto, 2012: 22; see also Keßler, 2006).

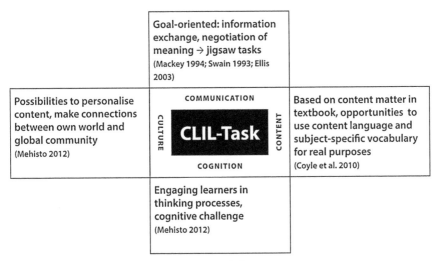

Figure 2:   Applying the 4Cs model to CLIL task design

5.2   CLIL tasks: An example

In the following, a CLIL task will be presented that was used in the study. It was designed on the basis of an excerpt of a text taken from the textbook used in both classes. This was done in order to assure that the task included general content and skills with which the learners were familiar, even though they had not yet worked with the text itself. The text deals with the ethnic structure of the Australian population. It provides brief historical information about Indigenous Australians[2], Europeans and Asians in Australia and explains their respective roles in the Australian population (for an example, figure 3). In addition, a graph is provided that shows the distribution of the population by ethnic descent (European 92%, Asian 7%, Indigenous 1%). The activity given in the textbook is: *Describe the ethnic structure of the Australian population* (Appleby et al., 2007: 152).

---

2   In the textbook, the name Aborigines is used. This is why the learners also use this name in their task-based interactions (see chapter 5.3)

The Asians

When in 1850 the Chinese heard that there was gold in Australia, they started to arrive to try their luck. (…)

It was not, however, until the 1970s, when [sic] Asians began to arrive in larger numbers, often as refugees. This large-scale migration became possible after the Australian government had stopped its 'White Australia' immigration policy.

Today, there is still a large influx of immigrants from the neighbouring Asian countries. The main countries of origin are China and Vietnam, but there are also many immigrants from Indonesia, Malaysia, Hong Kong, and the Philippines.

Figure 3:   Excerpt from the text 'The Australians', Diercke Geography Volume 1 (Appleby et al., 2007: 152)

This activity was adapted in a way that it would make it possible for learners to approach the content presented in the text through communicative interaction. At the same time, it was intended to challenge them cognitively and put a stronger focus on cultural learning than it originally allowed for. A jigsaw task was developed which learners were supposed to solve in groups of two or three. Each learner was given a part of the text, i.e. they had different pieces of information about the ethnic groups. No information was given regarding the distribution of the population by ethnic descent. The learners completed the task in 3 steps: they

1) read the text assigned to them and were asked to think about the percentage of people with, e.g., European heritage,
2) explained their choice to their partner(s), and
3) completed a pie chart together that illustrates the population of Australia by ethnic descent.

The spontaneous language produced by learners while they were performing the task was recorded, transcribed and analysed (The data were transcribed according to GAT 2 'minimal transcript' conventions (Selting et al., 2011; see Becker; Kupetz, Kupetz this volume)). The results of the analysis will be presented in the following section.

5.3   Using interactive CLIL tasks: Results

The results of the analysis show in how far the CLIL task leads to the kind of interaction at which it was targeted and initiates the intended learning processes. At the same time, using the linguistic means available to them at this point, learners "provide insights into the processes at work in their acquisition of a second language" (Nicholas, Lightbown, 2007: 46). This is shown in the following example, in which two learners are discussing the percentages they have assigned to the different groups of population in Australia:

Extract (1)

```
01   C1:   okay ehm what do you think (.) eh how many (-) european (-)
02         descents are (.) in australia? (-)
03   C2:   eh i think ehm that there are (.) twenty-five percent europeans
04         in australia.
05   C1:   =only? ((surprised))
06   C2:   yeah because i saw the number for the asian (.) immigrants and i
07         saw that there are just seven pro' percent (.) so i (-) didn't
08         think that ehm (.) there are so many europeans (--) because ehm
09         asia is also (.) ehm nearer (-) than europe to australia and i
10         think that the asian people (.) eh don't have so many reasons to
11         go to australia (.) because there i think in asia (.) generally
12         ehm (--) south there is a good life and good lifestyle but in
13         europe the people have more reasons to go (-) eh as immigrants
14         to australia and- yeah i just have twenty-five percent.
15   C1:   why do you think that?
16   C2:   yeah because ehm (---) europe ehm (1.5)
17   C1:   i think ehm many people from asia eh (.) from asia ehm (.) can
18         eh or should go because ehm (.) i think the life ehm in asia is
19         much harder than in european.
20   C2:   yeah ehm (-)
21   C1:   another point. ehm if eighteen (if)(--) ehm no if the eighteenth
           century the european travelled to ehm australia ehm i don't know
           how many thousand people ehm (.) travel but the (-) population
           grow-
22   C2:   yes;
23   C1:   and the twenty-three million australians are there (--) i think
24         (.) more than ten million are (.) or have (-) ehm (.) european
25         decs' (.) descens. (-) do you know what i mean?
26   C2:   yes, yeah i know ehm;
```

This extract shows that, as intended, the task leads to a high degree of meaningful interaction. Learner C1 does not accept learner C2's explanation, and the percentage he has chosen, and convinces him that more than 25% of the Australian population have to be of European descent. The two learners exchange information from the text and collaboratively negotiate how to draw a pie chart in order to come to a common solution. The extract also shows that the interaction is based on the content matter dealt with in the text and provides opportunities to use content language and subject-specific vocabulary for real purposes, such as comparisons or conclusions. Here, learners are still struggling with the pronunciation of the words *descendant / descent*, which shows that corrective feedback is necessary in open learning scenarios in the CLIL classroom. In addition, the extract demonstrates that the task challenges learners cognitively: they have to derive new information from the information they were provided with, using practical reasoning. They use language to hypothesize, to build arguments and to express disagreement, thereby constructing their own understanding (Coyle et al., 2010: 54). In addition, the learners have to transform "information from one form of representation to another" (Ellis, 2003: 7; Kupetz, Kupetz, this volume) when transferring information from a text to a pie chart, which, at the same time, promotes the development of subject-specific skills.

The data show that the cultural dimension also plays an important role during task performance. Having decided what percentage they would assign to the different groups of population, learners were presented with the percentages given in the textbook. They were surprised to find out about the reality of population distribution in Australia, which led to different reactions. In extract (2), it led to emotional reactions of the three learners involved, who showed empathy for the plight of the Indigenous Australians.

Extract (2)

```
01   C4:   that's much more europeans; (4.0)
02   C5:   ehm yes, that's very surprising.
03   C4:   yeah;
04   C5:   yes (.) we thought it's not so much.
05   C4:   yes, (-) i don't thought there are so much europeans.
06   C3:   yeah i thought there are much more abo' (-) aborigines. but (-)
07         there's just one procent (---) and it's very less.
08   C5:   yes ehm yeah and because of the british colonies (--) it's not
09         so much (---) and that's ehm (-) very (-) that's not good
10         because ehm that shows that many of the aborigines dies (--) and
11         (.) that's (-) not very,
12   C3:   in my opinion, it's not fair (--) because it's eh australia and
13         there first were aborigines and then all (.) more british people
14         came and the europeans.
```

What the learners express here reflects their ideas of social justice and sensitivity towards the importance of human rights (line 12), which are important elements of a critical cultural awareness.

Other learners also thought there were more Indigenous Australians and showed similar reactions. Extract (3) demonstrates how they make connections with their own world, in order to make sense of the facts they were presented with:

Extract (3)

```
01   C1:   i haven't thinked that ehm (.) only one procent of the
02         aborigines survive;
03   C2:   i'm a little bit shocked (--) because i thought (-) i mean (.)
04         ninety-two percent of europeans that's (.) a lot (.) it's (1.0)
05         eh (--) there are,
06   C1:   =that's twenty-one million yeah
07   C2:   =there are hardly aborigines and (-) yeah (-) just one percent
08         of aborigines and seven percent of asians (-) and ninety-two of
09         europeans. (.) what do you think about that?
10   C1:   i'm also shocked. (.) one pro (.) procent that's are (.) hmm
11         it's a (-) when i compare some (-) eh every aborigines in
12         australia (-) so many people live in darmstadt.
```

In this case, learner C1 sets the number of Indigenous Australians in relation to the population of the German city of Darmstadt (line 12), which is close to the town in which the learners' school is located, in order to make the comparison seem more immediate.

In another example, the learners hypothesise why there are not as many Asian people as they had initially concluded from the text:

Extract (4)

```
01   C3:   ehm i don't know (-) maybe there are not SO many asians and (--)
02         ehm i don't know it.
03   C5:   because when you look a movie about (.) australia there are eh
04         much more (.) ehm people who look like (.) Europeans and- (-)

[...]

43   C5:   and maybe ehm it's why (.) also there are not so many asians
44         because ehm they are only tourists (--) and they aren't then the
```

```
45          inhabitants. and we have eh also many asian tourists here (--)
46          when you look at the big cities (-) and maybe that's the result.
47     C3:  the reason why;
```

The conclusions that the learners draw here are based on their own intercultural experience (line 3). But, as the interaction continues, the learners also appear to draw on the stereotype of the "Asian tourist" (line 6) in order to make sense of the result. Furthermore, extract (4) shows that the learners respond to each other not only on the level of the content of the message that needs to be conveyed, but also on the level of its form. This becomes obvious as learner C3 gives corrective feedback to learner C5 by finishing his sentence correctly (line 09), and it points to the opportunities tasks offer for learners to learn from each other both on the level of content and language.

As regards the cultural dimension, the above examples illustrate the learners' developing intercultural skills and their "ability to bring the culture of origin and the foreign culture into relation with each other" (Council of Europe, 2001: 104). This process is also related to the concept of a "third space" (Hallet, 2004; Rutherford, 1990), in the course of which elements of different cultures merge, thus enabling new positions to emerge.

All in all, the learner interaction elicited through task performance shows that the task achieved its aim. It made it possible for learners to approach content through communicative interaction and the resulting performance indicates that it stimulated learning processes at the levels of communication, content, cognition and culture.

5.4   Reflecting on the results

With regard to the use of CLIL tasks in the classroom, a look at the data presented above may raise the question of how we are to deal with the diversity of results such a task-based approach can yield. The learners' performance provides evidence that the task initiates heuristic processes, i.e. it encourages them to learn by discovering things for themselves. What learners discover can be regarded as an important stepping stone in the learning process. It may later be theorised, so the results of task-based work can serve as a basis to continue work in the classroom. As for the intercultural learning processes that become evident in the data, a possibility would be to encourage learners to critically compare the societal status of Indigenous Australians and minorities in Germany. In this context, the use of the name 'Aborigines' in the textbook could be contrasted with the name 'Indigenous Australians' and discussed with regard to issues of cultural hegemony. Concerning the occurrence of stereotypes, an approach could be to create an awareness of learners' existing perceptions of other cultures (Byram et al., 2002: 27f.).

In a more general approach to raising learners' meta-affective awareness (Mehisto, 2012: 20) and encouraging them to think critically about their own learning, learners can also be asked to reflect on a given task. This was also done in the study presented here. After they had completed the task, the learners were asked to reflect on the task and to give spontaneous feedback. Interestingly, their spontaneous reactions and comments show that they were well aware of some of the intended learning processes and outcomes. This is illustrated in the following example:

Extract (5)

```
01   C11:   i think it was an interesting task because (.) ehm normally in
02           the books there (.) is a percentage written down and you only
03           read it and don't think about it (.) and say oh there are (.)
04           less but you (-) you don't really think about ehm, (.)
05   C12:   yes and you ehm (.) maybe you (--) keep it better in mind when
06           you eh (.) thought a longer time about it and disCUSS (.)
07           discussed and ehm (1.0) and then you have it (-) oder so
08           ähnlich ehm thought a longer time about this (.) ehm percentage
09           and then maybe you know it for weeks and not for hours.
10   C11:   yes and i think ehm so you can (-) build your own mind about it
11           and when you read it you know this percentage and ehm (-) don't
12           see (.) how you really THINK about it and, (.) yes i think it
13           was a good task because you also speak with another person and
14           so you can improve your English very well.
```

In their comments, learners C11 and C12 compare the task-based work they have experienced to regular work with the textbook (line 2). What they express here demonstrates that they view learning through active involvement, as it took place during task performance, as more effective and sustainable, because it makes them think about the issues at hand more thoroughly (line 6; 10) and thus not only leads to a deeper understanding but also helps them to remember information more easily (line 9). At the same time, they see the advantages which interaction in the target language may have for their language learning (line 14). In this sense, working with CLIL tasks can also be seen as promoting more global goals, as it enables learners to take responsibility for their own learning and, this, in turn, fosters learner autonomy.

6. Conclusion

The integration of tasks into the CLIL classroom can create learning scenarios that enrich content and language learning in many ways. The study presented here clearly shows that the use of CLIL tasks can lead to positive results. More research, focusing on different CLIL subjects, learner groups and task types, is required before we can make reliable statements and predictions about the effect of CLIL tasks. Future studies could also include tasks with an additional focus on form in order to promote the use and acquisition of specific target language features (Long, 2009; for examples, see Coyle et al., 2010, Lyster, 2007).

The data presented here are based on only one task and provide only limited evidence. Nevertheless, they can be relevant for, and complementary to, current research into CLIL, as they provide insights into the complex learning processes that take place during task-based work in the CLIL context. They show that a task-based methodology, that brings together content, communication, cognition and culture as four key components of CLIL, provides many opportunities for learners to engage in communicative interaction. It makes it possible for learners to use the target language to co-construct meaning while dealing with content (Coyle et al., 2010: 153), and has the potential to initiate and sustain inter-cultural learning processes.

References

Appleby, Matthew et al. (2007). *Diercke Geography for Bilingual Classes.* Volume 1. Braunschweig: Bildungshaus Schulbuchverlage.

Bogaert, Nora, Van Gorp, Koen, Bultynck, Katrien, Lanssens, An, Depauw, Veerle (2006). 'Task-based language teaching in science education and vocational training', in Kris Van den Branden (ed.), *Task-based Language Education: From theory to practice.* Cambridge: Cambridge University Press, pp. 106-28.

Bonnet, Andreas (2012). 'Towards an evidence base for CLIL: how to integrate qualitative and quantitative as well as process, product and participant perspectives in CLIL research', *International CLIL Research Journal* 1, 4: 66-78.

Bonnet, Andreas, Breidbach, Stephan (eds) (2004). *Didaktiken im Dialog. Konzepte des Lehrens und Wege des Lernens im bilingualen Sachfachunterricht.* Frankfurt am Main: Peter Lang.

Breidbach, Stefan, Viebrock, Britta (2012). 'CLIL in Germany – results from recent research in a contested field of education', *International CLIL Research Journal* 1, 4: 5-16.

Byram, Michael (2008). *From Foreign Language Education to Education for Intercultural Citizenship. Essays and reflections*. Clevedon: Multilingual Matters.

Byram, Michael, Gribkova, Bella, Starkey, Hugh (2002). *Developing the Intercultural Dimension in Language Teaching: A practical introduction for teachers*. Strasbourg: Council of Europe.

Council of Europe (2001). *Common European Framework of Reference for Languages*. Cambridge: Cambridge University Press. 10 October 2013, retrieved from http://www.coe.int/lang.

Coyle, Do (2002). 'Relevance of CLIL to the European commission's language learning objectives', in David Marsh (ed.), *CLIL/EMILE – The European Dimension: Actions, trends and foresight potential*. Public Services Contract DG EAC: European Commission, pp. 27-8.

Coyle, Do (2005). *CLIL Planning Tools for Teachers*. 10 October 2013, retrieved from http://de.slideshare.net/gorettiblanch/theoretical-clil-framework.

Coyle, Do, Hood, Philip, Marsh, David (2010). *CLIL – Content and Language Integrated Learning*. Cambridge: Cambridge University Press.

Dalton-Puffer, Christiane (2008). 'Outcomes and processes in content and language integrated learning (CLIL): current research from Europe', in Werner Delanoy and Laurenz Volkmann (eds), pp. 139-57.

Dalton-Puffer, Christiane (2011). 'Content and language integrated learning – from practice to principles?', *Annual Review of Applied Linguistics* 31: 182-204.

Delanoy, Werner, Volkmann, Laurenz (eds) (2008). *Future Perspectives for English Language Teaching*. Heidelberg: Carl Winter.

Doughty, Catherine, Williams, Jessica (eds) (1998). *Focus on Form in Classroom Second Language Acquisition*. Cambridge: Cambridge University Press.

Ellis, Rod (2003). *Task-based Language Learning and Teaching*. Oxford: Oxford University Press.

Ellis, R. (2009). 'Task-based language teaching: sorting out the misunderstandings.' *International Journal of Applied Linguistics* 19/3, 221-246.

Hallet, Wolfgang (2004). 'Bilingualer Sachfachunterricht als interkultureller Diskursraum', in Andreas Bonnet and Stephan Breidbach (eds), pp. 141-52.

Hallet, Wolfgang (ed.) (2010). *English CLIL – Getting started für Klasse 5 und 6*. Stuttgart: Klett.

Hallet, Wolfgang (2013). 'Aufgaben- und Materialentwicklung', in Wolfgang Hallet and Frank G. Königs (eds), pp. 202-09.

Hallet, Wolfgang, Königs, Frank G. (eds) (2013). *Handbuch Bilingualer Unterricht. Content and Language Integrated Learning.* Seelze: Klett & Kallmeyer.

Keßler, Jörg-Ulrich (2006). 'Negotiation for intercultural meaning in secondary school EFL-classrooms: Australia – a project', in Werner Delanoy and Laurenz Volkmann (eds), *Cultural Studies in the EFL Classroom.* Heidelberg: Winter, pp. 183-94.

Larsen-Freeman, Diane, Anderson, Marti (2011). *Techniques and Principles in Language Teaching.* Oxford: Oxford University Press.

Lightbown, Patsy M., Spada, Nina (2013). *How Languages are Learned.* Oxford: Oxford University Press.

Long, Michael H. (1996). 'The role of the linguistic environment in second language acquisition', in William Ritchie and Tej Bhatia (eds), *Handbook of Second Language Acquisition.* New York: Academic Press, pp. 413-68.

Long, Michael H. (2009). 'Methodological principles for language teaching', in Michael Long H. and Catherine Doughty (eds), *The Handbook of Language Teaching.* Oxford: Wiley-Blackwell, pp. 373-94.

Lyster, Roy (2007). *Learning and Teaching Languages through Content. A counterbalanced approach.* Amsterdam/Philadelphia: John Benjamins Publishing Company.

Mackey, Alison (1994). 'Targeting morpho-syntax in children's ESL: an empirical study of the use of interactive goal-based tasks', *Working Papers in Educational Linguistics* 10, 1: 67-89.

Mackey, Alison (1999). 'Input, interaction and second language development: an empirical study of question formation in ESL', *Studies in Second Language Acquisition* 21: 557-87.

Marsh, David, Coyle, Do, Kitanova, Stefka, Maljers, Anne, Wolff, Dieter, Zielonka, Bronislawa (2005). 'Report of central workshop 6/2005: CLIL QUALITY MATRIX', in Marsh, David (ed.) (2005). *Project D3 – CLIL Matrix – Central workshop report 6/2005* (Graz, 3-5 November 2005). European Centre for Modern Languages, 6, pp. 5-9, retrieved from http://archive.ecml.at/mtp2/CLILmatrix/pdf/wsrepD3E2005_6.pdf.

Mehisto, Peeter (2012). 'Criteria for producing CLIL learning material', *Encuentro* 21: 15-33.

Meyer, Oliver (2010). 'Towards quality-CLIL: successful planning and teaching strategies', *pulso* 33: 11-29.

Nicholas, Howard, Lightbown, Patsy (2008). 'Defining child second language acquisition, defining roles for instruction', in Jenefer Philp, Rhonda Oliver and Alison Mackey (eds). *Second Language Acquisition and the Younger Learner: Child's play?*. Amsterdam: John Benjamins, pp. 27-51.

Nikula, Tarja, Dalton-Puffer, Christiane, Llinares, Ana (2013). 'CLIL classroom discourse – research from Europe', *Journal of Immersion and Content-Based Language Education* 1, 1: 70-100.

Pica, Teresa (2002) 'Subject-matter content: how does it assist the interactional and linguistic needs of classroom language learners?' *Modern Language Journal* 86/1: 1-19.

Rutherford, Jonathan (1990). 'Interview with Homi Bhabha: the third space', in Jonathan Rutherford (ed.), *Identity: Community, culture, difference*, London: Lawrence and Wishart, pp. 207-221.

Selting, Margret et al. (2009). 'Gesprächsanalytisches Transkriptionssystem 2 (GAT 2)', *Gesprächsforschung - Online-Zeitschrift zur verbalen Interaktion* 10: 353-402.

Speidel, Ann-Cathrin, Dietz, Philipp (2009). *Prisma Bilingual: The human senses – your ears and eyes*. Klett Biologie: 8. -10. Schuljahr. Stuttgart: Klett.

Swain, Merrill (1993). 'The output hypothesis: just speaking and writing aren't enough', *The Canadian Modern Languages Review* 50, 1: 33-9.

Swain, Merrill (2000). 'The output hypothesis and beyond: mediating acquisition through collaborative dialogue', in James P. Lantolf (ed.), *Sociocultural Theory and Second Language Learning*. Oxford: Oxford University Press, pp. 97–114.

Theis, Rolf, Thimann-Verhey, Susanne, Wallmeier, Franz-Josef, Wicke, Martin (2009). *Geschichte und Geschehen – 19th century*. Schülerbuch. Stuttgart & Leipzig: Ernst Klett Verlag.

UCLES (2011). *Teaching Geography through English – A CLIL approach*. Cambridge: University of Cambridge ESOL Examinations.

Wesche, Marjorie (2002). 'Early French immersion: how has the original Canadian model stood the test of time?', in Petra Burmeister, Thorsten Piske and Andreas Rohde (eds), *An Integrated View of Language Development. Papers in honor of Henning Wode*. Trier: Wissenschaftlicher Verlag Trier, pp. 357-79.

Wolff, Dieter (2005). 'Approaching CLIL', in David Marsh (ed.) (2005). *Project D3 – CLIL Matrix – Central workshop report* 6/2005 (Graz, 3-5 November 2005). European Centre for Modern Languages, 6, pp. 10-25, retrieved from http://archive.ecml.at/mtp2/CLILmatrix/pdf/wsrepD3E2005_6.pdf.

Fremdsprachendidaktik / Foreign Language Pedagogy
inhalts- und lernerorientiert / content- and learner-oriented

Herausgegeben von / Edited by Gabriele Blell und Rita Kupetz
Mitbegründet von / Co-founded by Karlheinz Hellwig

Band 20 Marcus Reinfried / Laurenz Volkmann (Hrsg.): Medien im neokommunikativen Fremdsprachenunterricht. Einsatzformen, Inhalte, Lernerkompetenzen. Beiträge zum IX. Mediendidaktischen Kolloquium an der Friedrich-Schiller-Universität Jena (18.-20.09.2008). 2012.

Band 21 Friedrich Lenz (Hrsg.): Bilinguales Lernen. Unterrichtskonzepte zur Förderung sachfachbezogener und interkultureller Kompetenz. 2012.

Band 22 Anke Stöver-Blahak: Sprechen und Vortragen lernen im Fremdsprachenunterricht. Interpretativ, kreativ und ganzheitlich mit Gedichten. 2012.

Band 23 Joanna Pfingsthorn: Variability in Learner Errors as a Reflection of the CLT Paradigm Shift. 2013.

Band 24 Sylke Bakker: Fragen des Assessments aus Sicht von Englischlehrkräften. Empirische Annäherungen durch qualitative Inhaltsanalysen. 2013.

Band 25 Carmen Becker: Portfolio als Baustein einer neuen Lernkultur. Eine empirische Studie zur Implementierung des Europäischen Portfolios der Sprachen. 2013.

Band 26 Rita Kupetz / Carmen Becker (eds): Content and Language Integrated Learning by Interaction. 2014.

www.peterlang.com

www.ingramcontent.com/pod-product-compliance
Lightning Source LLC
La Vergne TN
LVHW092008050326
832904LV00002B/17